ABOUT THE AUTHOR

Ingo Swann (1933-2013) was an American artist and exceptionally successful subject in parapsychology experiments. As a child he spontaneously had numerous paranormal experiences, mostly of the OBE type, the future study of which became a major passion as he matured. In 1970, he began acting as a parapsychology test subject in rigorous and tightly controlled laboratory settings with numerous scientific researchers.

Because of the success of most of these thousands of test trials, major media worldwide often referred to him as "the scientific psychic." His subsequent research on behalf of American intelligence interests, including that of the CIA, won him top PSI-spy status.

Ingo's involvement in government research projects required the discovery of innovative approaches toward the actual realizing of subtle human energies. He viewed PSI powers as only parts of the larger spectrum of human sensing systems and was internationally known as an advocate and researcher of the exceptional powers of the human biomind.

To learn more about Ingo, his work, art, and other books, please visit:
www.Ingoswann.com.

ABOUT THE EDITOR

Elly Flippen was born into the family of artist, astrologer, and Remote Viewer Ingo Swann. Through her time with Ingo, Elly gained unique insights into his meticulous personality, spontaneous "supranormal" experiences, and the lively community of visitors who frequented his home. She has been deeply involved in preserving and chronicling her uncle's multifaceted legacy as an author, creator, and pioneer in perception and consciousness exploration.

She facilitated her mother's donations of Ingo's artwork to the American Visionary Art Museum, the Leslie Lohman Art Museum, One Archives at USC, and Edgar Cayce's A.R.E. She and her mother have also given his archives to the University of West Georgia (UWG) and One Archives at USC.

To inspire further research into the depths of human consciousness, Elly and her mother have established fellowships and scholarships at UWG.

She wrote, edited, and provided the art direction for the book **Stardust Highways: Ingo Swann's Art of Entertaining**, which showcases not only Ingo's artistic abilities but also his flair for cooking and entertaining.

She manages the X account @estateingoswann and website ingoswann.com, with the hope of inspiring future generations to embark on their own journeys into the mysterious wonders of the human biomind.

WHY DO WE FEEL THERE IS MORE TO US THAN WE, OR ANYONE, KNOWS ABOUT?

A COLLECTION OF INGO SWANN'S SUPERPOWERS OF THE HUMAN BIOMIND
ESSAYS EXCERPTED AND EDITED BY HIS NIECE ELLY FLIPPEN

A BIOMIND SUPERPOWERS BOOK
PUBLISHED BY

Swann-Ryder Productions, LLC
www.ingoswann.com

  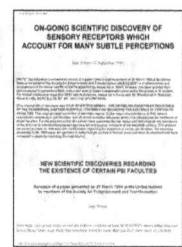

Copyright © 2024 by Swann-Ryder Productions, LLC. All rights reserved. No part of this book may be used or reproduced in any manner whatsoever without written permission. First edition BioMind Superpowers Books.

For more information address: www.ingoswann.com.

Cover art: **Flock of Birds** © Moritz, **Silhouette** © GDJ, and **Birds** © OpenClipart-Vectors from Pixabay.

ISBN-13: 978-1-949214-35-2

The content presented herein is for informational purposes only and is based on Ingo Swann's perspective and interpretation of the subject matter. Neither the editor, the publisher, nor any associated parties shall be held responsible for any consequences arising from the opinions or interpretations expressed within this book. Although the editor and the publisher have made every effort to ensure that the information in this book was correct at press time and while this publication is designed to provide accurate information in regard to the subject matter covered, the editor and the publisher assume no responsibility for errors, inaccuracies, omissions, or any other inconsistencies herein and hereby disclaim any liability to any party for any loss, damage, or disruption caused by errors or omissions, whether such errors or omissions result from negligence, accident, or any other cause. Fair use is a use permitted by copyright statute that might otherwise be infringing. All rights and credit go directly to its rightful owners. No copyright infringement is intended.

WHY DO WE FEEL THERE IS MORE TO US THAN WE, OR ANYONE, KNOWS ABOUT?

A COLLECTION OF INGO SWANN'S SUPERPOWERS OF THE HUMAN BIOMIND ESSAYS EXCERPTED AND EDITED BY HIS NIECE ELLY FLIPPEN

**TRYING TO FIT INTO THE REALITY WE THINK IS
THE ONLY REALITY.**

-- Ingo Swann, Everybody's Guide to Natural ESP

CONTENTS

---

[01] Editor's Note

[13] Author' Note

[19] Exordium

[35]   What Untapped Potential Lies Within Us?

    [37] Para-Speak

    [65] Awareness

    [85] Perception

[117] Peroration

EDITOR'S NOTE

Within the pages of his book, **Reality Boxes and Other Black Holes in Human Consciousness**, my uncle, Ingo Swann, a renowned explorer of the depths of consciousness, wrote about how most individuals tend to operate from what they know, or what they believe they know, without much interest in what they do not know. This mindset is a shared characteristic among those trapped within the confines of their own "reality boxes"[1]—some of whom have neglected to cultivate four essential human elements: sympathy, empathy, human-heartedness, and intuitive connection. Nevertheless, these elements, he said, are constantly experienced, even if only on an individual

---

[1] Our individual thinking processes are shaped and guided by our personal frames of reference, constructing a unique mental framework that determines our perception of "reality." This reality is subjective and limited, as it is confined within the bounds of our own understanding. We each have our own "box," comprising of our beliefs and experiences, which may not align with the objective truth. Our perception is limited by these self-made boundaries, creating a personalized version of reality that may not necessarily reflect the true nature of things.

level or at a subconscious level.

This innate ability to intuitively link with oneself plays a crucial role in why so many individuals feel there is more to themselves and their existence than can be accounted for by their daily lives. And why he wrote it is not unusual for one to ask, "What, is THAT it? Is that all there is to life, to MY life, to MY existence?" The simple truth, he explained, is that humans are capable of so much more, beyond the constraints of conventional understanding.

Based on substantial evidence, he argued, without our uplifting powers of intuition and insight, our species would be lost. He pondered, just imagine removing sympathy, intuition, and insight from the human equation—where would we be? Down the tubes, as it were, he said, and not too long after Day One of human existing.

He also wrote about how today we live in a seemingly endless glut of information—from the mundane to the utterly profound. We are constantly bombarded with data, facts, opinions, and beliefs. And yet, despite this saturation of knowledge, he said, there is still so much that remains unknown, unexplored, and mysterious. It is tempting to assume that everything worth knowing has already been identified and documented.

Still, this assumption can lead to another dangerous one—that there are no vacuums or black holes in our collective understanding of the world. But true seekers of knowledge, he noted, understand there are always hidden layers and alternate perspectives waiting to be discovered. We often rely on the information fed to us through official channels and mainstream sources, he maintained, but we must also acknowledge the existence of unofficial information nestled within occult, esoteric, and mystical traditions. When we combine these different sources of knowledge, we realize there is still so much left to uncover.

And burrowed within this much to be uncovered, he said, is our psychic faculties. Ingo's interpretation of the term psychic went beyond its popular connotations of "Psi" abilities, things we call clairvoyance, telepathy, and precognition;[2] they are merely forms of connectiveness or connecting, he wrote. Rather he saw "psychic" as a vast and intricate system, one he referred to as the "psychic triad."[3] This triad is made up of three distinct "thinking processes," each one serving as an arm of a system. It is this triad, Ingo recorded, which serves as a mere prelude to the expansive journey of perceptual development.

The first part of the triad is immediately recognizable, for it holds within it the power of intellect and the humanoid process-talents of logical, analytical, and analogical thinking. These unique abilities, often lumped together under the labels of "reason" and "rationalism," are far more complex and powerful than their simplistic titles suggested.

They possess a depth and intricacy beyond ordinary reason, capable of producing extraordinary results that surpass anything mere rational thought can achieve.

---

[2] In the most simplistic terms, the abilities of clairvoyance, telepathy, and precognition can be described as follows: Clairvoyance is the ability to perceive beyond the range of ordinary perception. Telepathy is the phenomenon of communication between minds, a connection that transcends physical barriers. And precognition is the remarkable knowledge of future events, a glimpse into what is yet to come.

[3] In his book, **Resurrecting the Mysterious: Ingo Swann's 'Great Lost Work,'** Ingo goes much deeper into this topic.

In our culture, the intellect is often overlooked as being a product of psychic origins; it is not typically seen as having a connection to the "paranormal." However, in ancient cultures and certain Eastern beliefs, the intellect was recognized as being connected to what we today call "the supernatural."

Even contemporary scientists, who have delved deep into brain research and discovered the astonishing potential of electro-physical cells, now understand the physical brain by itself cannot explain the complexities of intellect, let alone the vast differences in intelligence among individuals and societies.

The second part of the triad is shrouded in obscurity, its once prominent features now concealed by the passing of time. In the last hundred years, its constituent parts have fallen out of favor within the context of modern psychology. They have been relegated to the shadows, overshadowed by the demands and expectations of various method psychologies.

Our understanding of them has been further diminished by the rise of behaviorism, which sought to reduce us to mere cause-and-effect response mechanisms with no other dimensions or complexities. Nonetheless, they remain and are made up of feeling, emotion, and sensing functions that can be grouped together under the broad term of sentiments.

Unfortunately, this term has become less popular in modern society and is seldom spoken, leading to a loss of understanding and connection to it. Regardless of the contemporary aversion to sentiments and what they represent, the sentiments are of extraordinary power and are intensely psychic.

On a different level, the second arm focuses on electric, electronic, and electromagnetic processes that control the physical human body. These processes are completely invisible and cannot be perceived by physical means, but they shape the development of the body. It's possible these processes are responsible for creating or at least influencing the direction in which the body will evolve.

The third arm of the triad is known as the intuitional arm, a mysterious and often misunderstood aspect. Intuition, in its purest form, penetrates the "invisible" realm, bearing witness to the ethereal "Inferno" of creation. Beyond the confines of our physical time and space, this function can glimpse at the weaving of fate and destiny for all things in existence.

Though vastly different from one another, these processes cannot function effectively on their own. It is only when they work in harmony, each fulfilling its unique purpose, that one can reach a heightened state of being, becoming then a "psychic humanoid," having unleashed what Ingo called our superpowers.

Throughout history as well as in modern times, there have been countless anecdotes of people experiencing the spontaneous workings of their superpower faculties: innate abilities that go beyond the limitations of time, matter, energy, and space.

These abilities involve a heightened level of awareness and perception, as well as elusive phenomena that are difficult to grasp or define. The transcending can be subconscious, subliminal, or conscious—or, perhaps, superconscious.

These occurrences attest to the undeniable existence of these innate abilities within us. All the same, it is crucial to differentiate between two types of interactions with these faculties: (1) spontaneous, uncontrolled experiences and (2) conscious, deliberate engagement with them.

The extensive historical record of our species reveals that certain societies tolerant of these powers allowed for the development of various forms of conscious interaction with them. This demonstrates the potential for harnessing and honing these faculties to achieve incredible feats beyond what we may think possible.

But to do so, we must, he said, have a context for them. The process of contextualization begins with creating a deep understanding of its components.

Without a solid understanding of its origins and principles, the triad may function erratically, leading to a multitude of inexplicable experiences that fill the archives of psychical research, parapsychology, and the pages of paranormal books and magazines.

To grasp this concept, we must first explore the intricacies of superpowers. These sophisticated abilities are composed of natural internal elements that can exist in three distinct states: active, inactive, or blocked. But before one can truly harness and utilize—and change the states of—these superpowers, one must first study the corresponding awareness spectrums that govern them.

Without a deep understanding of these spectrums, success in activating these powers will be limited. In essence, it can be encapsulated as:

1) No activation of awareness equals no recognition or manifestation of superpowers; and
2) Increased knowledge and expansion of awareness leads to heightened recognition and activation of superpowers.

● ● ●

In 1973, Ingo became deeply immersed in anomalous phenomena[4] research at Stanford Research Institute (SRI). It was there it became increasingly vital for him to break through new levels of understanding.

He knew he had to steer away from the overused and standardized concepts of parapsychology and psychical research that had become stale with convention.

Instead, he sought out innovative insights that would push the boundaries and bring about groundbreaking discoveries. In this way he found many significant concepts were being ignored, deemed unimportant or irrelevant.

As he continued the investigation, gaping holes in our understanding began to reveal themselves, highlighting the urgent need for new and innovative insights. Crucial information that had previously evaded us now demanded to be uncovered and understood.

The groundbreaking concept of Remote Viewing (the practice of seeking impressions about a distant or unseen subject) became the focal point of the research, serving as both its central pillar and a developmental core for understanding all other superpowers. This intense study lasted for a span of fifteen years, resulting in the creation of a new "map" that brought these extraordinary abilities to light.

This map, he said, is still in its early stages, subject to change and additions as time passes on into the future. Like a canvas waiting to be filled with vibrant colors and details, Ingo began creating a database of

---

[4] Situations or occurrences that goes against what is anticipated based on current rules and scientific knowledge, either through personal experience or observation.

essays, his and others, holding the potential, he hoped, for shaping a Brave New World, as the noble Aldous Huxley might have envisioned.

The construction of this database was intentionally left unstructured; no hierarchy or ranking of topics was determined. A vast array of issues must be addressed, he wrote, each holding a significant place within the larger picture of the superpowers. He saw this, what he called the **Superpowers of the Human Biomind** database, as a constantly evolving landscape just waiting to be explored. Ingo understood as individuals, with unique backgrounds and perspectives, it is natural for us to have varying intellectual and experiential viewpoints.

That is why he chose to construct his database as a vast collection of topics and essays, allowing readers to approach them one by one, potentially uncovering new layers of understanding.

Each piece surveys a specific subject, inviting readers to consider its intricacies and gain a greater insight into the topic at hand. This approach, he felt, catered to those seeking a nuanced understanding rather than a broad overview.

True comprehension is only attainable when information can be seamlessly woven together, he believed. And so, each essay in this database meticulously tackles a separate topic or subject, investigating its complexities and subtleties.

More than anything, Ingo felt it is not simply about comprehending the individual topics, but also about experiencing the interconnectedness of it all.

In this manner, his insightful explorations are documented in an array of books from thought-provoking treatises like **Resurrecting the Mysterious** and **Psychic Literacy** to intricate concepts such as

Secrets of Power I and II, Reality Boxes, Psychic Sexuality, and **The Wisdom Category,** to informative guides including **Everybody's Guide to Natural ESP** and **Your Nostradamus Factor.**

Ultimately though, Ingo thought, the psychic humanoid, with its complex and inexplicable nature, may be formed by not only a trinity, but also a quaternity, an octet, or even hundreds or thousands of individual parts.

As our collective knowledge and understanding of consciousness and perceptual growth advances in the future, new and astonishing discoveries may be made in realms that we cannot currently fathom.

Though, before one can attain this intellectual understanding, there must be a journey that goes beyond mere academic knowledge. It must be accompanied by the actual experience and reality of it.

These revelations can only be found within oneself and cannot be attained through external means.

We must embark on a deep exploration of our inner selves, he wrote, awakening our inherent abilities of awareness and perception to unveil these personal truths.

This task is solely ours to undertake, as no one else can do it for us.

It was amidst my own journey of self-discovery, I came to deeply comprehend the vital significance of awareness and perception.

Seeking further understanding, I turned to Ingo's provocative collection of essays in his **Superpowers of the Human Biomind** database.

Once in, I found a tangled web of ideas and concepts to unravel.

As I poured over them, to enhance their impact and clarity, I found myself editing, reworking, and reordering sections that pertained directly to my personal enlightenment.

As I extracted materials from these compositions, I had a sudden realization—why not compile my own selection of these profound reveries?

My goal then became to carefully select and curate a collection of works that embody the inquisitive voice within us begging the question: why do we feel there is more to us than meets the eye? A journey that begins with peeling back the layers of awareness and perception. And thus, this collection was born.[5] In publishing it along with my book **Conjunction.World**, I hope it serves as a launching pad for the testament to our limitless potential as human beings.

---

[5] The entire contents of Ingo's website **Superpowers of the Human Biomind** can be found as a free PDF download within the Empiricist page of the website ingoswann.com; in addition, a full set of his **Superpowers** essays can be found as a free PDF download on the website conjunction.world. As to Ingo's main sources of information for these essays, other than himself, he depended on the **Oxford Dictionary of the English Language**, **Webster's Seventh New Collegiate Dictionary** (1967), **Encyclopedia Britannica**, and **New Columbia Encyclopedia**. He often referred to them for the Latin or Greek origins of words and their definitions, sometimes even quoting directly from them. Any other sources Ingo used are referenced within the text itself.

THE MOST IMPORTANT THING TO REALIZE ABOUT ESP AND OTHER PSYCHIC FACULTIES IS THAT WE DO POSSESS THEM.

-- Ingo Swann, Everybody's Guide to Natural ESP

AUTHOR'S NOTE

It is widely accepted that those with inquisitive and analytical minds have a strong interest in matters of great importance. Yet, the areas in which such minds seem to land, science and philosophy, are heavily influenced by the social environments in which they exist; without support from these environments, neither can thrive. When we refer to "social environments," we are essentially talking about power structures within society.

Power, and maintaining it, is always the top priority within these structures. In simpler terms, power structures dislike information and knowledge that could challenge or weaken their authority and beliefs. Therefore, the determination of what is considered valid knowledge is often a societal concern before it's recognized by those in scientific and philosophical fields.

As far back as Francis Bacon (1561-1626) and his famous phrase "Knowledge itself is power," the connection between knowledge and power has been recognized. It is clear various power structures have always kept a close watch on emerging knowledge, either to support or disrupt their authority. This means societal power has always come first, with science and philosophy following closely behind—if they adhere to societal guidelines for exercising their knowledge. In this way, knowledge truly can be seen as power, capable of creating and maintaining it for those who possess it. Conversely, lack of knowledge or a deliberate withholding of certain types of knowledge results in disempowerment for those without it, the powerless, at the hands of those in control.

It is undeniably evident being aware and having power are closely intertwined. But it is not so clear which types of awareness hold more significance in terms of power dynamics.

To truly grasp the impact of this relationship, one must consider how increases in functional awareness at an individual level could potentially affect societal systems and their hierarchies of power. A closer examination of these power structures reveals their continued existence relies on maintaining a certain level of unawareness among the masses.

Aware, in this context, describes states of consciousness or conditions that directly relate to factors of power. In THIS sense, it's understandable why those in positions of knowledge management for societal power structures may see "being alert and attentive, vigilant and constantly watchful" as their greatest difficulty. The avoidance of this can be achieved in various ways and on different levels, but one highly effective method is simply to suppress and eliminate all discussions about awareness from constructive discourse.

By doing so, knowledge of proactive awareness cannot trickle down to those with less power. This in turn keeps us from considering and discussing how astonishing, amazing, wonderful, creative, energetic, visionary etc. we actually are.

In this vacuum, our existence as individual beings is shaped and defined by our senses. Our sense of self or identity is intricately connected to how we acknowledge, develop, and utilize our sensing systems. On a conceptual level, this operation requires the human brain to decipher and breakdown information into conscious elements that form our understanding of the world. Like a key unlocking a door, our physical senses allow us to interact with the physical universe, but it is our brain-mind system, our bio-mind, that truly connects us to it.

Every perception from our surroundings is filtered through this intricate system, molded by our environment and education before reaching our conscious awareness. It's like a puzzle, each piece handpicked and placed by our own experiences and perceptions, ultimately shaping how we interpret and make sense of the world around us.

As humans, we are aware that through repetition and emphasis, something can become more prominent in our minds. This process is called "learning," and it involves creating new neural pathways for specific data and information. Over time, this repeated exposure can lead to assigning meaning and importance to something that may not deserve it or may not have even existed in the first place. It is not unfounded to say our species has both aspects of intelligence and ignorance within us.

One cannot deny the darker aspects of humanity are undeniably captivating, leading to the development of ways and means to exploit them for their economic potential. This widespread fascination has become a valuable commodity, complete with a market of producers and consumers. Our negative aspects have proven to be so charismatic that when they and our positive ones are discussed together in sort of dichotomous contexts, the negative ones attract all the attention. Or at least various amounts of attention wander away from our positive aspects and over to the lascivious excitements promised by the negative aspects. Sadly, it seems, little can be done to change this reality, except to acknowledge that our positive qualities do not quite measure up to the allure of our negative ones.

But let us not disregard the positive ones, for they hold just as much power. These superpowers are the abilities that often go unnoticed and unappreciated, yet still possess incredible strength—such as insightful thinking and deduction, intuition that foresees outcomes, problem identification and solving, and that type of clairvoyance, sometimes referred to as "hunches" or "gut-feelings," that can perceive what is invisible to the physical senses. This author even goes further, elevating the act of thinking to the status of a superpower, recognizing its distinction from thoughtlessness, particularly in moments of great ignorance. And perhaps one of the greatest superpowers, often overlooked, is Caring—an innate ability that can bring about immense positive change and influence.

This concept suggests all humans are carriers of these remarkable abilities and their limitless potential—much like how all humans carry the genetic makeup of humanity within themselves. Secrecy exists, obviously and covertly so. Human superpowers, often called exceptional human experiencing, also exist. The conventions of secrecy do not want the superpowers to be developed into useful advantages. Therefore, conventional situations following the supposed advantages of secrecy make clever and successful efforts to distort appreciation of superpower evidence.

This distorting disables and alienates constructive development of superpowers. A superpower vacuum thus comes into existence within the species that possesses raw superpowers and so the superpowers cannot develop any muscle. Therefore, super-secrecy can proceed—and claim victims among any number of conventional situations that otherwise might oppose it in conventional terms.

The principle reason for this is that our species possesses the superpower of cleverness.

When mobilized to even a near-perfect degree, it can outwit just about everything, certainly including conventional situations.

Hugo Swan

EXORDIUM

In the past, this writer had the unique opportunity of personally getting to know several "natural psychics" and in doing so took the time to deeply study their autobiographical outpourings. The allure of these individuals sparked a deep fascination within me, and my goal was clear: to uncover the commonalities within their unique personalities.

During the 1960s, when I first encountered it, the prevailing belief in psychical research, and later parapsychology, was that mediums and psychics had little in common beyond their tendency towards egotistical displays. Their personalities were seen as vastly different from one another.

Most parapsychologists didn't pay much attention to the individuals themselves, as their focus was on exploring "Psi phenomena" rather than studying people. The topic of personality seemed almost inconsequential in comparison. In this manner, one common excuse that was often given to ME, was that the psychics had difficulty articulating themselves and therefore their messages were hard to understand.

At any rate, as researchers, it is our duty to look

beyond surface level issues and try to understand the person behind them. Despite their varying abilities, the psychics all shared one important factor, which upon closer inspection, became easier to identify.

Everyone in the group possessed a vast and expansive perspective, however, it was evident that each had their own unique approach. It was, though, this undeniable overarching characteristic that united them as a distinguishable collective. It was implied that their broad understanding of the world may be linked to their Psi abilities and could potentially shed light on their sense of detachment from various aspects of the surrounding world. Yet, this state also brought with it a sense of isolation, as they struggled to find connection with those who could not see the world through the same lens as them.

The feeling of being an outsider, once seen as a barrier, had made things easier. It could be associated with a variety of respectable sources, all connected to the concept of social alienation. One particularly notable source was Colin Wilson's highly praised and widely revered book, **The Outsider** (Houghton Mifflin Company, 1956).[6] Within its pages, Wilson eloquently dissects the intricate "anatomy" of The Outsider. Still, he does not solely focus on the outsider as a traditional misfit, he also highlights what sets the outsider apart and makes them unable to fit in. Translating Wilson's observations, one central issue faced by outsiders is their expansive perspective exceeds the narrow social boundaries they are expected to conform to.

Wilson theorized, with considerable accuracy, that most social settings lack any visionary elements. He

---

[6] Ingo noted this book is "suggested reading" for anyone truly interested in the superpower faculties.

depicts this dearth of vision because of mainstream society's tendency to avoid addressing factors that may disrupt conventional social norms and equilibrium. Wilson's "visionaries" refused to conform to societal norms, earning them the label of "Outsider."

His book not only explores the mental struggles of these individuals, but also examines how social structures can stifle and limit their abilities—and it is this which leads us back to the subject of "natural psychics," and their ability to see things from a wide and expansive perspective. It is this worldview, this expansive perspective, which proved challenging for them when attempting to articulate their thoughts and experiences using the limited terminology and beliefs of modernist psychical and parapsychological concepts.

Surprisingly, despite the extensive research on Psi abilities, no one had ever asked a psychic to express their worldview in writing. Through my own conversations with numerous psychics, I discovered many—though not all—believed these superpower faculties were present within every person but remained dormant in most. This wasn't just a trendy, egalitarian idea for them—they could sense and feel this truth within the majority of the everyday individuals they encountered.

The concept of "EVERYONE" is more than just a collective term for the vast conglomerate of all people. It encompasses the essence of Our Species, from which each individual downloads their own unique experiences and perceptions.

Whether our faculties are dulled or heightened, they are inherent in our species, ingrained in our very nature. And so, it is here we find the gifted/un-gifted paradox versus powers inherent at the species level.

According to most dictionaries, the adjective GIFTED

is referred to as "having exceptional natural ability." But the origin of the word comes from the noun GIFT—which, beyond its meaning of "something given," also encompasses the idea of "a remarkable capacity or talent." Words that are like GIFT include FACULTY, APTITUDE, BENT, TALENT, GENIUS, and KNACK.

The action of giving a gift can also be described as "bestowing with some power, quality, or characteristic," although this usage is more commonly found in British English. Upon examining the definitions provided by various dictionaries, it becomes apparent that a gift is not simply an isolated object or concept. Rather, it can be understood as containing a composite of dynamic synonyms—a blend of faculties, aptitudes, bents, talents, genius, and knacks that result in the overall state of being gifted.

When it comes to giftedness, FACULTY refers to the natural or sometimes learned ability for a specific accomplishment or task. Therefore, one could say giftedness is a culmination of different combinations of inherent faculties, skills, talents, genius, and abilities that are in an active state. Conversely, if these combinations of innate factors remain unused or inactivated, then the manifestation of giftedness would not be possible.

Which leads us to consider the word "faculty." At its core, FACULTY embodies the idea of capability and personal aptitude. Yet, it also encompasses a wide range of physical and mental abilities or functions. Diving even further, some sources suggest that FACULTY can refer to individual components of the mind itself, each with its own unique purpose and role within the workings of our consciousness. Perhaps then, the concept is not simply one "thing" but a mosaic of various faculties working in tandem to explain all realms of mental phenomena.

And in terms of giftedness, a common issue that often arises is the question of who possesses superpowers, and who does not. This concept, handed down through tradition, attempts to categorize individuals based on their perceived level of intuition (the ability to "just know" something) or "extrasensory" perception (beyond the realm of "normal" perception). But such a black-and-white view fails to capture the true complexity and variety of human experiences and abilities.

Since ancient times, certain individuals have stood out from the rest of the population as "naturally gifted" in abilities such as shamanism, clairvoyance, mediumship, and intuition. Naturally, these gifted individuals have received a great deal of attention and recognition. However, what is less noticeable is that this attention towards the gifted takes away from the general masses who do not possess such gifts.

This creates a "basic reality" where psychic powers are seen as exclusive to a small percentage of gifted people and not available to the larger majority of the non-gifted. As a result, modern thought in the Western world has formed around the idea that one must be born with psychic abilities and cannot attain them through learning or training.

In our modern world, the notion of obtaining superhuman abilities through nurturing may seem far-fetched and fantastical. But in ancient India, it was believed these abilities, known as Siddhis in Sanskrit, could be learned and developed through instruction and devoted practice. To some, the teachings and practices of India may have seemed strange or unbelievable, but to others, they were a gateway to unlocking the limitless potential of the human bio-mind and bio-body. The concept begs the question of what else we may have disregarded from ancient wisdom.

Despite the modern belief that only those who are gifted can possess superpowers, there exists an approved exception. It involves the rare circumstance of an un-gifted individual suddenly, and often unexpectedly, gaining access to psychic abilities—whether temporarily or permanently.

It is not uncommon for individuals to experience a traumatic event, such as falling on their heads or receiving a forceful blow, and then discovering newfound psychic abilities that were previously nonexistent. In some cases, even those who were naturally un-gifted can undergo unusual mystical experiences, intense psychological catharses, or altered states that result in at least some level of psychic prowess.

Therefore, the notion that only inherent gifts determine one's possession of psychic capacities is not as concrete as it may appear.

While it may seem that all the excitement and attention is reserved for those gifted with psychic or Psi abilities, a closer examination reveals even the un-gifted experience their fair share of these mysterious events.

Through in-depth analysis and statistical data, it becomes clear a significant portion of the un-gifted population has also had experiences with spontaneous anomalous phenomena. Considering this larger scale, it is worth considering the possibility there is a much deeper and more complex picture underlying the narrow focus on the gifted few. Perhaps there is an intricate web connecting all individuals, gifted or not, in a grander scheme of things.

And with this, a major question arises: Whose faculties are already active, and whose are innate? Those who possess natural psychic abilities clearly have both innate and active faculties.

But these innate factors must also exist within those who do not possess such abilities; otherwise, it is hard to imagine how a blow to the head or an altered mental state could activate them. And even within this larger population, such factors must unconsciously dwell within individuals, as they seem to occasionally and spontaneously "turn on" in some people.

To fully understand and grasp this concept, we must shift our focus to what seems to be inherent in our species, and therefore would be present in everyone. Let us hypothesize that our species possesses a lengthy sequence of innate factors or abilities. This can be represented by the following diagram, where each "0" represents a specific innate faculty.

000000000000000000000000000000000000000000000

It is possible there are numerous innate faculties within us, perhaps in the hundreds or even thousands. We can theorize that most, if not all, of these innate faculties are downloaded into each individual of our species.

Regardless, only a select few of these faculties may actually be activated and utilized, while the rest remain dormant or potentially blocked by societal norms and conditioning. This can be visualized as such: "!" represents an active faculty, "*" represents a dormant one, and "X" represents a socially suppressed or desensitized one.

000000000000000000000000000000000000000000000
XXXX*!!XXXXXX***!!!***XXXXXXX**!**XXXX***!**

The diagram above is like a glimpse into the inner workings of the human bio-mind, hinting at the vast complexity and potential that lies within. It suggests the existence of forty-eight innate faculties, though it is likely there are many more waiting to be discovered. Of these forty-eight, only seven are currently active and utilized by most individuals. The remaining twenty lay dormant and inactivated, waiting for their chance to emerge. Another twenty-one have been desensitized or blocked by societal norms and expectations, resulting in a partial shutdown of their capabilities.

Despite the assumption that much is understood about our species, the reality is that what remains UNKNOWN looms like a dense fog, filled with countless unexplained mysteries. This fog is often overlooked or dismissed, as people prefer not to dwell on such uncertainties.

Nonetheless, the complications arising from this fog are undeniably real. To begin to navigate through this thick fog, one must first acknowledge its existence and be willing to face the unknown. It becomes clear that what we do NOT understand or even know about our species far outweighs what we do know. In fact, our understanding of ourselves is but a fraction of the larger picture that remains shrouded in the mists of uncertainty.

The enigmatic nature of our existence is made even more astounding by an equally astonishing truth: in moments when we cannot fully grasp or comprehend our being, our species always finds a way to create and conjure a form of "understanding." It is a remarkable feat, this human ability to construct meaning and explanation from the seemingly incomprehensible.

When discussing the nature of our species, conventional beliefs often start by focusing on the bio-bodies that are said to make us up. It is undeniable that human bodies are a marvel of biological engineering, whether through natural evolution or artificial means. But what sets our species apart is the abundance of elements and faculties that extend far beyond mere survival on Earth.

Our species has been strategically over-endowed for survival, both individually and collectively. This separates us from all other species, who are equipped with only the essentials for survival. This distinction begs the question of where exactly our species originated from, as there is clearly a significant gap between us and all other life forms on Earth.

And in this way even though our species being blessed with a superabundance of faculties, many of them are underutilized for basic survival. Yet, generation after generation, these essential abilities are passed down and continue to manifest in individuals in unique ways. Like sparks from a fire, the signature elements of our innate potential flare up and are experienced.

The true existence of these fundamental elements can be easily determined not only by their spontaneous eruption. The exceptional essentials not only burst forth on their own, but many societal subgroups within our species actively suppress and inhibit the development of these innate faculties—essentially admitting to their existence while simultaneously denying them support and growth.

One possible way to conceptualize this is to speculate that our over-endowed species has the ability to harness one hundred percent of its powers. Despite that, societal norms often discourage utilization of more than a mere ten percent. This begs the question—why would a species have such incredible abilities if they were never meant to be used? In other words, what purpose does the foundation for these faculties serve if they were never intended to be activated in the first place?

Social structures are built upon a foundation of differences, creating a hierarchy that is often artificially maintained. This allows for the ease of stratification to occur, with some individuals being favored over others based solely on their perceived differences. Unfortunately, this means factors of sameness within our species are often marginalized or completely ignored. Be that as it may, upon closer examination of these sameness factors, one can begin to understand that they are the core, or "cake," while the differences are merely the "frosting."

At the individual level, a profusion of diverse and intricate "frosting" designs are likely to be encountered. And as we explore the underlying factors that unite us as a species, we begin to uncover the fundamental foundations upon which every member of our kind is built. One cannot help but notice the countless ways in which these commonalities branch out into unique variations, often influenced by cultural and social upbringing rather than inherent natural differences. As the saying goes, nature provides for us while we, as humans, carve out our own boundaries among what is given. Another telling detail is that with some level of understanding about our species' shared traits, it becomes clear these factors tend towards the extraordinary, leading us down paths of awe-inspiring and the truly remarkable.

And it is these boundaries, carefully crafted and defined, which are shaped by one's level of understanding and familiarity with a subject, one's KNOWLEDGE. This is especially evident in the modern cultural West, where KNOWLEDGE is often defined as "the fact or condition of knowing something through experience or association."

In spite of that, there exists a subtle discrepancy between (1) the definition of knowledge gained through experience and association and (2) the concept of innate knowledge. The discrepancy centers on the definition of INNATE, which is first described as "inherent: belonging to the essential nature of something." A second definition follows, stating it can also originate from the mind or intellect rather than experiences. This inconsistency holds significant importance, most notably for those well-versed in the twentieth century's widespread denial of innate KNOWLEDGE.

During this epoch, the notion of innate human "instincts" was occasionally, albeit begrudgingly, acknowledged. The idea of innate KNOWLEDGE, however, was often met with resistance and caution, as it bordered on forbidden topics such as inspiration, intuition, divine revelation, clairvoyance, telepathy, and extrasensory perception—all of which seemed to defy logic and reason. Furthermore, the concept of innate KNOWLEDGE posed a complex and puzzling question: how and why would KNOWLEDGE, out of all things, be naturally embedded within the human species?

But in terms of KNOWLEDGE, on average, most assume merely learning about something will somehow result in a product. And if this does not transpire, then most also assume the fault is with the learning. But in better fact, learning must fall into and interact with whatever it DOES fall into. If the desired result is not achieved, then the chances are quite good that the learning has fallen into grounds inadequate or unprepared—fallen into grounds that cannot really accommodate or nourish its seeds.

In Western concepts of the mind, there is a common trait that values rote-learning and step-by-step methods for understanding. While this approach has proven effective in many areas, it can also be limiting, like painting by numbers. There are far more profound and powerful forms of creativity within all human beings that may not always be awakened through these methods. This "mind-ground" of how-to tutorials is often hidden behind various teaching styles and learning myths, and even beyond the grasp of the student's own cognitive comprehension.

It must be made clear that no blame or criticism is being placed on any individual's mind-ground. Rather, it is crucial to recognize the existence of a situation concerning superpower activation that has gone without examination and appreciation for its true significance. Although, this is not an uncommon occurrence.

Many fields that demand efficient functioning also require diligent training of the mind before any actual results can be seen. In fact, as one takes a step back and calmly assesses the situation, the question arises— what exactly constitutes a properly prepared mind?

There is no simple answer readily available for this predicament. The task of preparing one's mind for a multitude of scenarios is a complex undertaking. Nevertheless, it is much simpler to render the mind unprepared for various situations or even completely unprepared altogether. This can be achieved by confusing the mind or limiting its function to basic tasks, particularly regarding societal expectations and conventional notions of intelligence. Here we encounter a principal clue that probably has great relevance to the concept of preparing the mind to interact with the superpower faculties.

As we explore this clue, it is crucial to acknowledge the significance of social norms and average intelligence in shaping our societal structures. These concepts serve as the foundation upon which stability and productivity are built. Still, it has been proven—as demonstrated by some of the leading sociologists—these larger ideas are actually rooted in smaller, more specific realities. These "smaller realities" act as building blocks for the "bigger-picture," influencing and shaping our understanding of social norms and intelligence.

Constantly, we are faced with the task of navigating within smaller frames of reference. These microcosms exist and should not be disregarded or dismissed. Nonetheless, it is important to recognize these smaller-pictures can be manipulated and crafted in a way that excludes or even prohibits contact with larger realities.

Upon further reflection, it becomes clear that if our superpowers are meant to exist within a larger context, then confining ourselves to these smaller contexts can hinder their true potential and act as invisible barriers to their full functionality

If this were to occur, one's mind, primed only for smaller scale situations, may need to expand its horizons and incorporate larger contexts for the seeds of superpower abilities to truly thrive and prosper. The concept as a whole may initially seem incongruous or unconventional. Yet, there is ample precedent to support such an idea, easily accessible and ready to be utilized.

When considering the contrast between smaller- and bigger-picture scenarios, it becomes apparent there are countless levels and layers in between. Naturally, there are numerous complexities that can arise when discussing these differing perspectives. In broad terms, bigger-picture factors encompass those that are universal to our entire species, while smaller-picture situations focus on localized elements within our species. It is like zooming in on a map, where the bigger-picture shows the layout of an entire city, and the smaller-picture reveals the details of a single neighborhood.

It is unquestionable that our species possesses a universal intelligence system, ingrained within our "hard drives." However, upon closer examination, it becomes clear this intelligence system cannot function to its full potential without the support of at least two other universal "hard drive" systems: a comprehensive network of sensing mechanisms and an intricate system for recognizing meaning. These additional systems cannot simply be composed of localized "software programs" but must utilize a combination of "hard drive" components that encompass the entire species as well as each individual's unique downloads and experiences.

For those interested in learning and development, it is not uncommon to have the instinct to deconstruct and eliminate anything that appears to be getting in the way. After all, if the superpowers of the human bio-mind are part of a universal system rather than a localized concept, it makes sense to reject, abolish or demolish any smaller-picture ideas or thoughts.

Still, this approach presents a problem.

The act of rejecting something is itself a product of a smaller-picture mindset. While it may require some mental effort to consider, it can be easily demonstrated that smaller-pictures can be identified by what they reject, ignore, overlook, rationalize away, or simply lack knowledge about. In other words, attempting to achieve a bigger-picture understanding by following the same pathways that lead to constructing smaller-pictures is challenging at best.

An amusing, yet perplexing aspect of our species is

our tendency to focus on smaller-pictures rather than the bigger-picture. Many individuals become agitated and hostile when confronted with smaller details, and some even go to great lengths to discredit them. This behavior can be compared to jousting at windmills if one does not understand the criteria for constructing a smaller-picture.

The real question is: what makes a smaller-picture small and how can it be identified as such? After all, to escape from something, one must have a clear understanding of what they are trying to escape. It's like trying to navigate through a maze without knowing its layout; it only leads to confusion and frustration. This brings about an intriguing question: if we only use a small fraction of our innate faculties, what untapped potential lies within us?

WHAT UNTAPPED POTENTIAL LIES WITHIN US?

PARA-SPEAK: THINGS CHANGE

Outside of traditional science, vital forms of psychic research have emerged. Since 1935, a diverse range of phenomena have been studied and explored under the umbrella of the label parapsychology; noting here the Greek origin of the prefix "para-" refers to something located next to or alongside something else.

Through parapsychology, new concepts, ideas, terminology, and frameworks have been developed; this combination of slang, jargon, and colloquialisms creates a unique form of language that I have come to call "para-speak."

While appropriate for parapsychology, it does not apply to other mainstream scientific fields.

The exclusion of parapsychology from the realm of science, I believe, is a form of apartheid, a systematical isolating of Psi and its related fields from mainstream study. This segregation, I argue, stems not from empirical evidence but rather from philosophical biases entrenched in modern mainstream scientific thought. Consequently, parapsychology and its unique discourse evolved largely in isolation from established scientific paradigms.

This disjunction gave rise to several nuanced phenomena that are rarely acknowledged or explored within the broader scientific community.

One striking example of this subtle dynamic is found in the sociology of science itself; an exploration reveals that scientific comradeships actively impose restrictions against integrating concepts and terminology, para-speak, from parapsychology into mainstream scientific dialogue. These prohibitions serve to further entrench the divide, perpetuating a cycle of exclusion that stifles innovative thought and interdisciplinary exchange.

Any scientist who dared to propose cross-over concepts faced professional backlash due to the strict enforcement of this embargo. And even now, this embargo stands strong. As a result, there were several social consequences that stemmed from it.

1) Mainstream sciences often dismiss psychic phenomena, using derogatory terms like superstition, abnormal, and hallucinatory. In the field of psychiatry, these abilities are considered signs of mental illness and are attributed to distorted or damaged psycho-physical causes.
2) The mainstream sciences have deliberately avoided using any language or terminology that could be interpreted as related to psychic, parapsychological, or paranormal phenomena. Therefore, the use of non-pejorative terms in this context is often referred to as para-speak.
3) The integration into mainstream scientific research of para-speak is not allowed, meaning any papers discussing Psi must be written in a way that avoids any hint of overlap between the two fields.
4) When individuals, or even the public, wish to

discuss the enigmatic and mysterious aspects of life without negative connotations, they are compelled to employ ideas and terminology from the field of parapsychology.

Wrapped in layers of complexity, this four-part situation manifests one significant consequence: the unending perception that mainstream sciences and parapsychology are locked in a state of mutual exclusivity.

This view has been entrenched over time, with no allowance made for cross-pollination of concepts or terminology by the dominant scientific community. As a result of this schism, another significant consequence has emerged: a marked DECREASE in the exchange of ideas and findings between traditional science and the realm of parapsychology.

Consequently, it has become widely accepted—perhaps even taken for granted—that any potential revelations regarding the so-called paranormal would occur solely within the confines of parapsychology itself, effectively sidelining them from mainstream scientific inquiry.

Conversely, it is assumed mainstream sciences will not yield discoveries relevant to what is deemed paranormal phenomena since they lack both the inclination and the historical precedent for engaging in such lines of research. Thus, at first glance, this dichotomy presents a profoundly stagnant tableau: an insular world where parapsychology caters exclusively to its practitioners while conventional science remains firmly within its own domain—existing in parallel yet never converging.

BUT! Nothing ever stays the same, AND all things do change.

The main sciences, no matter what opinions one may hold about them, are essential for continued discovery. They may experience peaks and valleys, periods of stagnation and gaps in knowledge, but over time they gather extensive data and undergo major paradigm shifts.

In my own opinion, the rate of discovery in these fields has been significant and rapidly increasing since the 1950s—to the point where the implications of these discoveries may be beyond our ability to fully comprehend in certain areas. Furthermore, many of these implications reach beyond established frames of reference, not only within the scientific community but also in terms of societal and cultural beliefs.

If we allow ourselves to ponder the ever-growing wealth of knowledge amassed by mainstream science, it becomes nearly inconceivable that these disciplines would not inadvertently stumble upon breakthroughs that hold significant relevance to the enigmatic realm of "parapsychology."

Such discoveries could illuminate the central hypotheses that underpin our understanding of these extraordinary phenomena.

Thus, considering the rigid and long-established chasm separating parapsychology from conventional scientific inquiry, one can easily envision considerable professional challenges in bridging the gap between mainstream findings and the often-dismissed studies of parapsychology.

Should a connection between these two realms be forged, it is undeniable that parapsychology would undergo a profound transformation—if for no other reason than to reconcile itself with the colossal body of knowledge represented by mainstream sciences, far overshadowing the minuscule efforts traditionally associated with parapsychological research.

The implications of such an integration could redefine our comprehension of both fields, merging empirical rigor with the mysteries of human experience.

The future of Modern Parapsychology, a field often marginalized and overlooked, may hinge on its acceptance and integration into mainstream science. Perhaps the key lies in recognizing the potential discoveries within this field as relevant to human functioning as a whole.

For example, parapsychologists view telepathy and clairvoyance as unique forms of mental perception, and because of this, they have spent decades seeking to understand the underlying psychological mechanisms, the procedures and criteria that trigger or accompany these phenomena.

If such research were embraced and acknowledged by the scientific community, it could transform our understanding of human capabilities and potentially elevate parapsychology from a niche subject to an integral part of our collective knowledge.

From my personal experience and research, I have concluded there has been significant progress in the field of parapsychology.

Unfortunately, many parapsychologists tend to disregard this progress because it may not directly support their central hypothesis that Psi is a function of the human para-mind. As a result, the accumulated results in parapsychology are often deemed "not very robust" and considered unsuitable for repetitive experimentation.

This perpetuates the notion that Psi remains an elusive concept within the field, while theories about it are riddled with inconsistencies: One example of this that stands out to me is the perceptual phenomena related to Psi in parapsychology. Regardless of their para-mental source or cause, these phenomena undoubtedly involve elements of information transfer, acquisition, and processing. While the para-mental hypothesis cannot be dismissed, perhaps the more vivid and manageable issue at hand is actually related to information processes.

Psi as a concept related to the mind and Psi as a concept related to information are fundamentally distinct fields of study. While parapsychology has few information theorists, the realm of Information Theory and Applications is highly developed within mainstream sciences.

The field of study has a long history of expertise in comprehending the complex mechanisms of receptors, transducers, and signal-to-noise ratios. These scientifically termed components play a vital role in obtaining and interpreting information. Similarly, neurobiology has revealed that the human body is made up of receptors, transducers, and signal-to-noise decoders, which all contribute to the processing of sensory inputs, with some components seemingly responsible for Psi-like information gathering.

Thus, in certain respects, both information theory and the field of neurobiology have little connection to parapsychology; nonetheless, advancements in these disciplines are increasingly overlapping with concepts traditionally associated with parapsychology.

Sometimes, it's a matter of using different words that creates divisions between these realms.

Without knowledge of advancements in information theory and neurobiology, one may wrongly assume that conversations about Psi phenomena are only relevant to the field of parapsychology.

According to conventional wisdom, one might

expect that a significant shift in parapsychology would emerge from groundbreaking discoveries made within its own realm. Yet, this expectation has not materialized. Instead, it appears that when the established sciences expand their understanding of Psi phenomena—those mysterious and elusive events that defy easy explanation—beyond what parapsychologists have unearthed or are capable of comprehending, a transformative paradigm shift may occur.

This evolution could potentially overshadow parapsychology entirely, integrating it into a broader scientific narrative that leaves behind the limitations of its previous frameworks. Such a transition hints at a future where parapsychology is redefined, reshaped by insights gained through rigorous scientific inquiry rather than solely by its own explorations.

There are numerous topics that require discussion, many of which have already been addressed here. One significant point is that particular phenomena arise when a paradigm shift takes shape and starts gaining traction. One of the initial signs of this shift is that commonly used terminology, which once held substantial significance in the outgoing paradigm, begins to lose its impact as the new paradigm starts to crystallize. In some cases, it doesn't take long for well-known terms to end up forgotten and discarded.

As the mindsets that utilized these terms fade away, so too do the terms themselves, leading to their eventual obsolescence. This transition goes beyond simply determining whether certain words are currently "in" or "out," or deemed "politically correct."

Terminology functions as a vessel of knowledge; in other words, knowledge is organized in specific ways within a given paradigm, and each term not only conveys its own meaning but also reflects the structure of the underlying knowledge package.[7]

As new advances and discoveries are made, it becomes necessary to reorganize and restructure our understanding of the world. In these cases, old terms and concepts no longer apply, as they represent previous ways of thinking and understanding. Each knowledge package is defined by its key words—specific terms that are essential to grasp the concept at hand. And each knowledge package has a specific framework in which information is organized in a particular manner.

But, as knowledge evolves and changes, certain terms may fall out of use and become obsolete, no longer aligning with current understandings. This process can lead to a complete paradigm shift, where old knowledge is discarded in favor of new formats that incorporate the latest discoveries and advancements. Eventually, the old knowledge packages are relegated to obscurity, replaced by newer and more relevant ones.

In the study of parapsychology, the most used phrase during the twentieth century was ESP or "extrasensory perception." In present times, this term is mostly used by media outlets without proper understanding, and outdated parapsychologists who are not keeping up with current research.

As more discoveries are made about human functioning and new knowledge structures are created, the term ESP is becoming obsolete. This is because hard sciences have uncovered sensory receptors that were

---

[7] Ingo noted in the essays that over time, through teaching, experience, and educational techniques, most people learn to align their thought processes with accepted knowledge systems—knowledge packages—and reject those that are deemed unworthy.

previously unknown when the term was first introduced in the 1930s by Dr. J.B. Rhine. As a result, while these phenomena can still be studied within these new structures, they can no longer be considered as beyond the realm of normal senses, e.g., extrasensory.

There is a great deal of information and discussion surrounding ESP. Still, despite the amount of attention it has received, very little is understood about it. This lack of knowledge has led to parapsychology, the study of Psi and ESP, being labeled as the "elusive science."

The elusiveness of ESP, its very discovery and understanding, may explain why methods designed to teach and enhance it have not been very successful.

After all, it's difficult to teach something that is still largely unknown. If these methods did work effectively, we would likely see many highly skilled psychic humanoids already inhabiting our planet.

The previous comments were crucial for setting up a specific inquiry. Research on ESP phenomena has been ongoing for approximately one hundred thirty years, despite this however, the results have been more characterized by ambiguity rather than breakthroughs. This begs the question: why has this been the case after such an extensive amount of time? What factors have contributed to this outcome?

From 1973 to 1985, I was involved in a well-supported and dedicated project to study the human abilities associated with ESP. Even back in 1973, it was clear to some that parapsychology was struggling or even considered a lost cause.

We needed to understand why this was happening and find possible solutions, so we launched a multidisciplinary investigation with contributions from various experts in their fields.

As more information was unearthed, it became

apparent parapsychology, despite its endeavor to appear broadbrush, not only eluded understanding, but also remained secluded in its own realm. It was confined within its own infra-social boundaries, unable to connect with the vast expanse of global science and philosophy. Instead, it operated as a self-contained paradigm with its own unique terminology, concepts, theories, and patterns of behavior.

This self-isolating mindset can be traced back to the initial rejection of Psi research by mainstream science. Even with early attempts to integrate Psi phenomena into the scientific community, this endeavor has been met with resistance and opposition from traditional science. Be that as it may, the pursuit of integration continues in contemporary parapsychology, while being hindered by the reluctance of science proper to embrace it.

The long-term consequence of this situation was that parapsychology and ESP research became separated from mainstream science, leading them to create their own paradigms for studying ESP phenomena. This framework began to take shape around the time of World War I and solidified during the 1950s, with little alteration in fundamental principles since then.

Over time, this separation resulted in a lack of communication between the isolated parapsychology paradigm and the broader scientific community. As a result, advancements within parapsychology remained largely inaccessible to conventional science, but conversely, parapsychology also failed to incorporate developments from other scientific fields. In essence, crucial channels for information exchange between ongoing scientific research and the isolated field of parapsychology have not been established.

As but one example, somewhat amusing in its contradiction: while ESP is the focus of parapsychology, the study does not delve into perception itself. That kind of research falls under the purview of perceptual scientists in the proper sciences, who do not investigate extrasensory forms of perception.

Thus, while parapsychology focuses on the ES part, it neglects the P part, while other sciences attend to the P part but disregard the ES aspect. In other words, while both parapsychology and mainstream sciences of perception acknowledge perception as a shared element, there is no direct communication between the two fields.

It is quite startling to see the extent of this issue. The two fields, although isolated and barricaded from each other, have developed different terms and theories for phenomena that are essentially the same. It is interesting to note that science proper has made more discoveries related to extra-sensory perception than parapsychology has.

Sadly, scientific language does not allow for the use of terms associated with ESP. Therefore, it can be difficult for the average person to understand that when neurobiologists refer to "bio-magnetic receptors," they are actually discussing the biological basis for dowsing, which is typically considered a form of ESP.

But the going here gets even a little rougher.

In the early days of parapsychology, before 1955, most of the fundamental ideas and concepts that continue to shape its thinking were already in place. One such concept was the belief that humans possessed only five physical senses, a widely accepted notion at the time. This belief led to the dominant idea in parapsychology that ESP did not have a biological basis in any of these five senses. In fact, it was necessary to create the term "extra-sensory" to describe this phenomenon—something beyond what could be explained by traditional senses.

This also meant ESP was seen as originating from a source outside of the physical body, independent of its material aspects. Thus, the term "extra-sensory perception" came to encompass a wide range of perceptions and abilities that could not be explained by traditional science or understanding.

Among the vast amount of evidence presented by parapsychologists, it is important to note that their findings point towards the human bio-mind's ability to acquire and transfer information.

However, this ability has been observed in contexts that go beyond our conventional senses—meaning outside of, or independent from, our sensory systems. While it can be proven that this information acquisition and transfer exists, its existence alone does not necessarily prove the underlying theory of extra-sensory perception. Nor does it confirm the involvement of extra-sensory bio-mind equipment in these processes. This raises further questions about the true nature and capabilities of the human bio-mind.

In the past, when science believed humans only had five physical senses, the concept of extra-sensory perception was barely accepted. In spite of that, it is now known humans possess many more senses than just five, and these additional senses are also physical in nature. Thus, the idea of extra-sensory perception may have always been contradictory.

In any event, many earlier parapsychologists—and a whole lot of scientists—objected to ESP on the grounds that ESP WAS an oxymoron. Thus, instead of limiting our thoughts to only Psi, psychic abilities, or ESP, it may be more precise to view the human mind as an intricate web of receptors which forms a complex network that discerns and governs our perceptions and understanding of the world around us. And this concept is not limited to a set of special abilities like ESP. Rather, it is a spectrum of broad capabilities that exist within all of us.

These latent abilities, often referred to as "super-faculties," go beyond the limitations of our cognitive consciousness and give rise to unlimited human potential.

As we continue to explore the connections between spirituality and physics through a multidisciplinary approach to consciousness, we can borrow more from scientific principles and move ourselves closer towards understanding how the "psychic entity" navigates both the physical and non-physical universes.

With the advancement of quantum physics, we have even greater opportunities to explain the powers of our bio-mind in a structured manner.

To put it simply, the extraordinary abilities of the human bio-mind are characterized by its capacity to surpass the limitations of space and time, as well as energy and matter.

It has been widely believed for the past two centuries that our powers and perceptions are confined to the laws of matter, energy, and time; however, this is not entirely accurate. The capabilities of memory and imagination, for example, go beyond these known laws. They are just a few of the many superpowers possessed by our species, although these attributes have not been traditionally recognized as such in the highly dominant ideology of the Modern Age.

Along with memory and imagination, which are inherent in all members of our species, there are also various forms of intuition (the ability to "just know" something) and telepathy (the ability to convey impressions of any kind from one mind to another) that are widely shared.

These first four "superpowers" may seem inexpiable by conventional beliefs based on matter and time, but they have been accepted as natural abilities. It is understood that these superpowers are the building blocks for creativity and inventiveness, two defining characteristics of our species. They likely exist along a spectrum of perceptual-cognitive abilities that all individuals possess to some degree.

This spectrum also includes other faculties that may not be as ubiquitous in their natural state but can be developed through focused efforts. Remote Viewing (the ability to see distant objects or events) is one such superpower that has been extensively researched and developed.

But societal factors and pressures can greatly impact our access to these superpowers, either positively or negatively. Furthermore, discussing these abilities within the confines of current or past social parameters is counterproductive in the larger discussion of their existence. These parameters are temporary and fleeting; the true nature of the superpowers should be examined beyond them.

The concept of superpowers transcends social constructs and varies in levels of understanding and knowledge. The potential for superpowers is inherent within our species and exists permanently. Every generation carries the capacity for these abilities, just as they carry our genetic traits.

Be that as it may, mainstream society has long discouraged and disregarded any research or discoveries related to the nature of superpowers. As a result, organized studies on Psi phenomena, the unknown factor in experiences that are not explained by "known" physical or biological mechanisms, have struggled to secure funding and gain recognition within academic circles.

This is because "they" do not want any progress in parapsychological understanding. This fear of Psi enhancing superpowers has existed for much longer than just the modern times.

In a society that actively rejects the development and understanding of Psi abilities, it would make sense for any information related to its potential factors to also be suppressed or obscured. This suppression is achieved through various means, from discrediting individuals who display Psi abilities to creating long-term gaps in knowledge and perpetuating cultural confusion around the subject. The mere mention of Psi is met with fear and skepticism, making it difficult for people to fully comprehend its complex and vast nature.

Even more abstract than the concept of Psi itself, however, is the idea of AWARENESS.

Our species' ability to be aware is crucial for our survival and success. Without awareness, we would simply react to stimuli with no ability to make purposeful decisions. It seems almost impossible to believe that something so integral to our existence could be so poorly understood.

Therefore, it is essential that we understand the dynamics of awareness. Unfortunately, there are gaps in our knowledge about this important faculty, which should not exist. This suggests a deeper underlying issue at play. And so, it becomes clear that different types of awareness and superpowers are not just connected, but fundamentally intertwined. Still, it is the single word AWARENESS we possess, with its concise and somewhat elusive definitions.

But what may not be immediately apparent is the intriguing evolution of its meaning over time. In modern dictionaries, tracing a word's etymology reveals that our current term AWARE is derived from the Old German-English GEWAR—described as "wary" and "watchful." The **Oxford Dictionary of the English Language** further notes that GEWAR was formed by combining GE and WAR, which can be translated as "to become wary" or "to become watchful or alert." Though, the element GE held multiple connotations, including "to have," but also "to be with."

Therefore, GEWAR likely meant "with wary," "to be within wariness," or even "to exist in a state of wariness-alertness."

These early interpretations suggest an alert and active awareness, constantly encompassing one's surroundings.

After discussing the origins of the words, most dictionaries label the definitions "wary" and "watchful" as archaic. This means that they are old-fashioned and no longer in use and using them may make one seem outdated. It is interesting to consider why these two terms, which encompass a wide range of awareness levels from street smarts to survival skills in various fields such as economics, military, diplomacy, and corporations, have been deemed obsolete and replaced with modern definitions for AWARE:

1) "Having or showing realization, perception or knowledge";
2) "Implying vigilance in observing or alertness in drawing inferences from what one sees or hears or learns."

In modern dictionaries, there are defined synonyms for the word AWARE:

- COGNIZANT: suggests having knowledge from personal experience or reliable sources.
- CONSCIOUS: implies a realization of the present existence of something, often with a sense of importance or preoccupation.
- SENSIBLE: indicates a direct or intuitive understanding, particularly of intangible concepts or emotional states.
- ALIVE: adds to SENSIBLE the connotation of heightened sensitivity towards something.
- AWAKE: implies an awakened awareness and alertness to something.

While the synonyms given above offer a fundamental understanding, they fail to explore the topic in greater depth.

First, the words listed as synonyms are not exactly interchangeable, or are only somewhat like each other. A synonym is defined as a word or expression in the same language that has an essential meaning that is identical or very close to another word or expression. Upon closer examination, it becomes clear there is a key difference between being aware and the given synonyms, when one considers that awareness must come before cognizance, consciousness, sensible, alive, and awake can be understood.

In other words, these synonyms are products of awareness. Without awareness as the primary factor, these secondary manifestations cannot occur. Stated more precisely, it's impossible to have cognizance or consciousness of something unless awareness of its components has already occurred beforehand. This idea is reflected in the definition of COGNITION: "The act or process of knowing, which includes both awareness and judgment."

The previous conversation is not just nitpicking—it has direct implications for understanding the concepts of causation and effect. The terms are all describing outcomes that originate from the state of being AWARE, and these outcomes may be erroneously perceived as primary causes.

Additionally, if we probe into the second definition of AWARE in a modern context, one could argue that "exhibiting awareness, perception, or understanding" are byproducts of awareness itself.

One could also say, in a more complete and elegant manner, that there must exist a fundamental principle of awareness. This principle is what forms the basis for all other definitions of awareness, as given above. However, if we consider this for theoretical purposes, we are ultimately left without a specific definition for what it means to be aware—unless we once again look at the supposedly "outdated" definitions of being "cautious" and "vigilant." If we do choose to consider these older definitions, we may wonder why they have gained this outdated status and why the secondary definitions have been adopted as the official and cultural meanings of being aware.

To understand the secondary definitions of AWARE, we can look at their commonalities. There are eight terms that represent these secondary manifestations: realization, perception, knowledge, cognizance, conscious awareness, sensitivity, alertness, and wakefulness.

One shared characteristic among these terms is that they can be seen as passive forms of awareness that can be influenced by external factors. This means one can be taught, guided, educated, or instructed on what to perceive or realize—and what not to realize.

On the other hand, being "wary" and "watchful" suggest a more pro-active approach for individuals. Yet, the underlying implication may not be immediately apparent unless one recognizes that it is challenging to control or influence large groups of people who possess these qualities.

If we were to imagine an ideal state of being wary or watchful, it would require unimpeded levels of awareness.

It's hard to believe actively aware individuals would consciously choose to ignore certain things. Therefore, the act of "unlearning" awareness can only be achieved through societal manipulation, using passive methods instead of active ones. This conditioning relies not on actual awareness, but on shaping its form for social purposes.

If one considers the above with patience, and as calmly as possible, one can see the eight terms—realization of, perception of, knowledge of, cognizance of, conscious of, sensible to, alive to, and awake to—are not variations of being aware, but rather qualities of the mind or thought process—which is heavily influenced by societal norms.

In other words, these are traits of the mind that can easily be shaped by structured systems of social control, like mind manipulation techniques.

If the above seems confusing, it becomes clearer once the definitions of the outdated word WATCHFUL and its synonyms are incorporated into the bigger-picture:

- WATCHFUL: "vigilant, wide-awake, alert, being on the look-out especially for danger or

opportunity."
- VIGILANT: according to most dictionaries, "suggests keen, unremitting, wary watchfulness."
- ALERT: "stresses readiness or promptness in apprehending and meeting danger or emergency or in seizing opportunity."
- WIDE-AWAKE: "applies to watchfulness for opportunities more often than dangers and suggests awareness of accurate meaning or of relevant developments and situations."

This definition of awareness is closely connected to various types of exceptional abilities. For example, a thorough analysis of recorded instances of natural extrasensory perception, instances such as telepathy, precognition, clairvoyance, and intuition, reveals that a significant number of them involve warning signals for potential danger. The remaining cases usually pertain to perceiving opportunities through these same means, again such as telepathy, clairvoyance, and intuition. These warnings and opportunities may pertain to present or future events.

Thus, it is important to recognize the unexamined connection between the vigilant and alert definition of "AWARE" and two essential functions of extraordinary abilities: (1) detecting danger and (2) recognizing opportunities.

One could theorize, although it is purely hypothetical, that our species is inherently designed to function as a complex and intelligent system. Evidence for this can be seen in the multitude of tools at our disposal: our abilities to sense our surroundings, make judgments, perceive, reason, and communicate through various means.

This "equipment" is innate within each individual,

and after birth, our development is greatly influenced by these innate factors. Truly, without the pre-existence of those various equipments, the human might be humanoid in body only, lacking any true humanity in other aspects. It is as if a vital piece is missing, leaving behind a mere shell of a being.

When we think of a "human being," we are not just considering the physical body, but also all its innate equipments—especially the mental equipment that makes up the mind.

While it may be difficult to determine which of these equipments hold more significance, there is one that stands out above the rest: without the arrays of awarenesses, it seems unlikely that the rest of the equipment would function properly or have much impact at all.

From the hypothetical musings above, we can surmise that every newborn babe enters the world with a complex and innate array of awareness, each facet ready to take on its designated role despite their initial unsteadiness. But as fate would have it, a child is not only born into the physical realm, but also into a unique set of circumstances shaped by environmental and social forces. This includes a specific set of knowledge packages tailored to their surroundings.

The vast panorama of our world offers countless possibilities for a child's birthplace and upbringing, each requiring the cultivation of different types of awareness units. Despite this, there are occasions where particular groups may impede or even work against the progress of different types.

This selective nurturing and suppression is also known as "social-cultural conditioning."

For instance, a child who is deemed "psychic" may not even understand the concept of being psychic, but rather just experience spontaneous shifts in perception and awareness.

We know that young children tend to have more open perceptions and awarenesses. When a child is able to articulate their experiences, they may ask questions that few can answer. But, if others start to notice and label the child as strange or weird, they may be encouraged to suppress these experiences or stop talking about them altogether. This means their once open perceptions become narrow and limited, conforming to what is considered "normal."

Unfortunately, this also means that they lose access to various states of perception and awareness, due to social conditioning.

In this way, the ultimate goal of this conditioning, though often imperfectly achieved, is to mold individuals who will seamlessly assimilate into society and uphold its norms. As time goes on, those nurtured awareness units will flourish while the suppressed ones gradually fade into dormancy or non-existence.

In terms of perception, the very act of, holds within it the potential for transformation into fully realized awareness, realization, and knowledge, depending on the state of one's other sensory faculties. Sadly though, our psychodynamics work to create margins that determine what we are capable of perceiving and being aware of; anything outside of those margins is either excluded or desensitized.

That is, our ability to perceive something allows us to gather information about it, while lacking awareness of something makes it impossible for us to perceive it and recognize any pertinent information related to it. In this way, it is safe to hypothesize that if something is not perceived, it remains invisible and beyond our grasp.

It is also plausible to consider—even if only as a

thought experiment—that dormant or underdeveloped senses may suddenly awaken in individuals who experience extraordinary abilities.

Thus, we can surmise awareness is not just a singular concept, but rather a multifaceted one that includes the specific categories of perception and cognition, which are activated by different sensory faculties.

It is a very common experience to have individual "realities," which are shaped by our direct experiences in life, as well as the information we absorb and adapt to through social conditioning.

Consequently, what may not be immediately clear about these individual realities is that they also set limits on our awareness and perception.

And without awareness, our perception of things can become questionable. When viewed through this lens, "gifted" individuals like shamans, psychics, and intuitives shine with a radiant aura of heightened awareness.

Their gifts are not just unexplainable abilities, but rather a fuller spectrum of perception that is constantly activated.

In essence, they possess an acute awareness of categories of consciousness.

For a visual representation of the contrast between those deemed "gifted" and those deemed "un-gifted," consider the following diagram. A "0" represents varying levels of specialized awareness, while the "!" signifies their activated state. The "*" represents an innate but dormant ability, while the "X" represents suppression or desensitization attributable to societal conditioning.

Un-gifted spectrum:
OOOOOOOOOOOOOOOOOOOOOOOOOOOOOOOOOOOO
XXXXX****!!XXXXX*XX!!********XXXXXXX

Gifted spectrum:
OOOOOOOOOOOOOOOOOOOOOOOOOOOOOOOOOOOO
!!!!!!!!XXXX****!!!!!!!!!!!!****!!XX

To this degree, awareness, perception, and information are closely intertwined, so much so that if one is removed, the other two also disappear. This interconnected trio forms a complex system that is vital to our understanding of the world.

While most people have a general understanding of what a system is, many do not realize that an individual's bio-mind is made up of various systems that work together to create their existence.

Therefore, it is possible to consider that awareness, perception, and information in-take and out-put are all part of specialized systems within the larger system of the human bio-mind.

But it does not stop there. In conventional terms, deducing is often not seen as a superpower. While it can be triggered by physical stimuli, it is largely a product of the mind rather than the five senses. Specifically, it is the result of ratiocination—a process of exact thinking and reasoning. It is important to note, however, that this term comes from Latin, RATIOCINATUS, meaning "to reckon."

The word "reckon" has a variety of imprecise definitions: counting, estimating, computing, calculating, considering, watching, and judging. Reckoning can involve determining something from a fixed basis, or it can occur without any clear basis at all—leaving us baffled as to how it works.

In these cases, we turn to the notion of KEN, which refers to the range of vision beyond just what our eyes can see. It encompasses perception, understanding, and knowledge beyond the physical world. KEN is a word deeply rooted in the Old Norse language, where it holds various meanings and connotations.

One of its core definitions, when translated into English, is a combination of "perceiving," "knowing," and "recognizing," with a special emphasis on the latter. Exploring further into the intricacies of Old Norse reveals that KENNING was not just a simple term, but rather a concept denoting "the inherent ability to attain direct knowledge or understanding without relying on rational thought or inference." This distinction sets it apart from the more limited definitions found in English translations.

KENNING embodies a profoundly deeper level of comprehension, one that transcends entrenched logic and embraces intuitive understanding.

This, of course, is our present understanding of INTUITION, a mysterious process that defies rational thought or logical inferences.

By way of an amusing example, for intelligence analysts skilled in deciphering multiple layers of meaning, the challenge lies not in their inferences rather in convincing their superiors and colleagues of their insights, as they often cannot be easily explained through reason or deduction.

It is important to note, while insight is highly regarded when it leads to success, it is defined as the "power or act of truly seeing and understanding a situation" through intuitive means. This requires an ability to grasp the essence and hidden complexities of things beyond what can be perceived by the senses or reasoned by the mind. In other words, by kenning.

MANY INDIVIDUALS SEEK A SIMPLE ANSWER, AN EASY SOLUTION TO THE COMPLEXITIES OF LIFE. HOWEVER, THESE SIMPLE ANSWERS OFTEN CONFINE US TO OUR CURRENT STATE, ALLOWING OURSELVES TO BE EASILY CONTROLLED AND MANIPULATED WITHOUT EVER EXPANDING OUR CONSCIOUSNESS. ACTUAL EXPANSION BEGINS WITH TRULY BECOMING AWARE AND HONING IN ON OUR DIRECT PERCEPTION.

IN THE QUEST FOR POWERS AND ABILITIES, TRUE ENLIGHTENMENT LIES IN BECOMING AWARE OF WHAT IS POSSIBLE.

MANY SEE THESE POWERS AS TANGIBLE THINGS, BUT THEY ARE ONLY MERE CONCEPTS UNLESS ONE'S MIND CAN GRASP AND HARNESS THEM.

THESE ABILITIES CANNOT MANIFEST WITHOUT THE ACTIVATION OF CORRESPONDING AWARENESS AND PERCEPTION.

AWARENESS: OUR SPECIES AS A SMART SYSTEM

In the glow of knowledge, if a school or institution devoted to cultivating the superpowers of the human bio-mind ever came into being, its core principles would revolve around understanding the intricacies and expansiveness of awareness. Not only would students learn methods for enhancing and expanding its various spectrums, but they would also rummage around in its entire panorama.

This topic of awareness is crucial for several precise reasons, specifically how:

1) The superpowers encompass the bio-mind's ability to transcend known limits and physical factors such as space, time, matter, and energy;
2) It is incredibly challenging to grasp how the bio-mind faculties can achieve this transcension without incorporating specific and essential forms of awareness;
3) Without awareness, the superpowers cease to exist;
4) Attempting to discuss and study the multitude of superpowers without recognizing them as

specific types of awareness modules will render them inactive; and

5) Those deemed gifted with "natural" superpower functioning also possess a natural activation of the corresponding awareness modules that allow them to utilize their abilities.

To my dismay, it is a commonly accepted fact within the enlightened world of parapsychology that our modern understanding and development of ideas like Psi have been restricted and confined too much. They are not given enough room to fully encompass all aspects of life processes.

In Western culture, these factors have often been reduced to simply "mental abilities of gifted individuals." In this way, attempts to train and harness these supposed mental abilities have largely failed. This begs the question: what if Psi factors are not mental abilities at all, but instead a complex system of functions within modules of awareness?

In this case, the key lies in identifying and activating the correct module of awareness. It becomes clear that mental abilities alone cannot achieve outcomes that are beyond their own conceptualization.

This concept can be approached from another angle. The extraordinary powers of the human bio-mind are undeniably remarkable. But more importantly, these abilities and their outcomes are based on specific modules of awareness. Without the activation of these modules, or if they have been dulled and rendered inactive, these abilities cannot reach their full potential.

Let us take a moment to contemplate the hypothetical scenario in which our species, and all individuals within it, lacked the diverse range of awareness spectrums that we possess.

Without these expansive arrays of consciousness, our being would be reduced to nothing more than an undifferentiated mass. In fact, one could eliminate the entire concept of a "mind" from the equation, leaving only a bio-physical entity capable of simple stimulus-response reactions, if even that. This raises the question: how different would our existence be without the richness and complexity of our various levels of awareness?

Looking beyond the surface of behaviorism, a deeper understanding of human history reveals that varying levels of awareness have always played crucial roles in our survival. This fact strongly suggests that any explanation or conception of the human "organism" must incorporate these elements of awareness instead of discarding them.

It is essential to recognize their significance—for we are far more than simply beings who respond to stimuli like toilet training and eating dirt when hunger strikes. Our complex existence goes beyond mere reflexes; it encompasses a rich tapestry of consciousness that shapes our actions and decisions.

As a tantalizing side note, there seems to be a phenomenon in some individuals where their awareness is fragmented and lacking—perhaps stemming from adhering to behavioristic beliefs.

Nevertheless, the importance of heightened levels of awareness is recognized by others—such as those with street smarts and those striving for success in the corporate world. Expanded awareness proves to be quite useful in these scenarios. After all, one cannot solely rely on a simple stimulus-response mechanism when trying to climb the rungs of a corporate ladder. It takes more than that to succeed in such a competitive environment.

The concept of awareness is a fundamental aspect of our species, serving as a crucial criterion for defining the impressive attributes of our intelligence. Without some level of awareness, no form of intelligence can exist or function. Even the basic tasks of toilet training require a certain level of intelligence and awareness to recognize and utilize designated facilities.

It is impossible to fully grasp the concept of intelligence without acknowledging its necessary companion—awareness.

When considering the relationship between awareness and intelligence, it becomes clear the two are inextricably intertwined. It is possible one cannot exist without the other, like two sides of the same coin. In an ethical and rational sense, it could even be argued awareness and intelligence are inherently linked.

Despite the vast amount of cultural, philosophical, behavioral, and scientific research dedicated to studying intelligence during the Enlightened modern period, unfortunately, there has been a notable lack of attention towards understanding awareness as its necessary counterpart—a significant gap in knowledge regarding awareness.

To reiterate, there is an old saying that something can occasionally be recognized by its voluminous or thunderous absence. The topic of awareness clearly falls into the category of subtle absenteeism. As but a few examples of prolific absenteeism, no reference to AWARENESS is found in any scientific compendiums or authoritative scientific resources.

The topic of AWARENESS is likewise absent from psychological compendiums and resources, while the term itself hardly ever appears in their indexes.

In the vast **Encyclopedia of Philosophy** (Macmillan, 1967), the concept of awareness is noticeably absent.

Despite its thousands of pages and in-depth exploration of philosophic theories and studies, this crucial term is only mentioned five times in the cumulative index. This fact raises questions: Is awareness being deliberately marginalized?

The absence of any substantial entry on awareness speaks volumes about the nature of philosophical thought and its priorities. As another, perhaps less-than-pleasant thought, one potential explanation for the lack of emphasis on AWARENESS in esteemed philosophical perspectives could be that venerated philosophers, like sociologists and behaviorists, may not require copious amounts of it.

As we return to the abundantly intriguing topic of parapsychology, it becomes clear that the multitude of subjects and theories are all connected by one common thread: awareness.

This elusive concept takes on many forms and states and is at the core of every aspect of "para-" normal research. Surprisingly, despite its significant role, there is no mention of awareness in any official catalog or list of terms related to psychic or parapsychological studies.

It seems this crucial component has been overlooked or ignored in the grand scheme of things. From telepathy to clairvoyance, each category of Psi can be traced back to a specific form or level of awareness. Our understanding and acknowledgement of this fundamental element, however, remains, quite alarmingly, absent from academic discourse.

What all of this adds up to is the subtle concepts of AWARE and AWARENESS are shrouded in a thick veil of taboo, so much so that they are not even acknowledged as being off-limits. This creates a double taboo, making the subject of awareness an ultra-taboo topic.

Throughout history, any attempts to explore this topic have been met with relentless deconstruction and condemnation, distorted by omnipresent fear and punished mercilessly. Any organized study of it has also been systematically dismantled and erased from existence.

Nevertheless, pushing the study of awareness or lack thereof aside, it is worth entertaining the possibility our species is inherently designed to be a highly intelligent system. Our very makeup suggests as much: a complex network of awareness units, diverse forms of perception, faculties for reasoning and problem-solving, abilities for recognition and deduction, keen senses and sharp judgment, and various means of communication.

All these innate capabilities exist within everyone. And every experience and development after birth hinges on the existence of these innate factors. Without them, a human may possess only the physical traits of a humanoid but would lack the distinct qualities that make us truly human in every sense.

When the concept of a "human being" comes to mind, it encompasses not only the physical body but also all of its innate equipment, which is commonly referred to as the bio-body's "mind." The mental equipment of the bio-body is a complex system that is composed of various components, and determining their individual significance can be challenging.

One element, though, stands out above the rest. Without the arrays of awarenesses, it is unlikely that the other equipment would function properly or hold much value. Building upon this hypothesis, we could surmise that each newborn possesses these innate arrays of awareness, right from the start. Though they may be initially unsteady, they are nonetheless present and ready to activate.

With every birth comes not only the beginning of physical-mental life, but also an immersion into a complex web of circumstances. These circumstances are shaped by environmental and social influences, as well as the boundaries and limitations of knowledge within each unique set of circumstances.

Across the vast expanse of our world, there exists an endless variety of socio-cultural landscapes a newborn can be thrust into. Each of these landscapes demands the cultivation of specific types of awareness, while simultaneously discouraging or even rejecting others. It is a delicate balance between nurturing and de-nurturing that shapes who we become in this intricate tapestry we call life.

The idealized, yet often unstable, ultimate aim of this conditioning is to mold individuals who will eventually mature and seamlessly integrate into the established mental structures dictated by the societal norms. Even infants born with expansive ranges of consciousness, lamentably, are subject to the influences of nurturing and neglect.

As they grow, those who are nurtured experience an acceleration in their awareness capabilities while those who are neglected gradually become dormant or non-functional. The impact of this conditioning can be seen on these individuals as they navigate through life, shaped by the expectations and pressures of their environment.

As mentioned previously, the concept of awareness has not been extensively researched. As a result, scientists and psychologists have also neglected to study the specifics of children's awareness.

On the other hand, experts who have delved into the field of developmental child psychology suggest that by the age of seven, crucial patterns of knowledge and beliefs have already been ingrained, shaping the child's future. This significant process typically occurs around this time in life, unfolding in two distinctive ways.

In one aspect, the fundamental classifications of information structures are firmly fixed and established to attain a seemingly unchangeable state. These include the precise formation and integration of specialized units of consciousness, which have been carefully cultivated to complement and reinforce the underlying patterns of information.

Inversely, the act of locking-down serves not only to secure and solidify the patterns that are locked-in, but also to block out any conflicting categories of information. This deliberate restriction extends beyond just physical barriers, but also includes a sort of mental blockade that prevents awareness units from accessing anything that contradicts what has been sealed away.

As this critical moment arrives, all the arrays of awareness units that do not align with the carefully cultivated ones are swiftly shut down and rendered inoperable.

It's like a door slamming shut, permanently blocking any opposing thoughts or beliefs from entering and disrupting the very carefully constructed world of understanding. The process is precise and efficient, leaving no room for error or doubt. This extraordinary occurrence has a dual effect that can greatly impact an individual's ability to retain and understand new information in the future.

As one grows, they will process information through the lens of their established patterns and beliefs, many of which were formed by the age of seven. These ingrained patterns then shaping their perception and understanding of the world around them.

Due though to societal influences and conditioning, many other wherewithals of thinking and processing information remain dormant and inaccessible to the individual. They have been forcibly "locked-out" and deactivated through the processes of being deprived of nurturing and molded by societal norms.

The point is one's awareness and the level of its functioning can be heavily influenced by external factors such as societal conditioning. In certain environments, only those forms of awareness deemed acceptable will be encouraged and nurtured, while any awareness deemed inappropriate, or unfitting will inevitably undergo a process of long-term suppression and deactivation.

We must now examine the definitions for AWARE and AWARENESS as two distinct categories: the active set and the passive set. In order to better understand these two categories, we will compare them side by side.

AWARE—AWARENESS

..
....
. . .

First Set
(archaic, active)
Watchful
Alert
Vigilant
Keen
Alive to
Awake To

Second Set
(modern, passive)
Realization
Perception
Knowledgeable
Cognizant
Conscious of
Sensible to
Alive regarding
Awake regarding

When taken together, there can be no doubt that the elements implicit in both sets paint a bigger-picture of whatever is functionally involved with the overall qualities of awareness and consciousness. Just the same, important and informative distinctions must be made between the two sets. The first set, with its archaic origins, discussed earlier, evokes a sense of an active inner state. It hints at a deep connection to one's own thoughts and emotions.

Alternatively, the second set implies a passive relationship to external factors such as situations, information, social norms, education systems, and so on. At first glance, one may think too much meaning is being drawn from these subtle differences. But there are vital clues that support these distinctions.

The passive set most probably functions only regarding the sum of what has been earlier acquired by passively being in-taken and imprinted. This can be seen in the major definitions of PASSIVE: acted upon by an external agency; induced by an outside agency; receptive to outside impressions or influences; receiving or enduring without resistance; submissive; existing without being active or open; lacking in energy or will; inert, latent; and non-volitional.

The replacement set therefore is suggestive of relationships to conditions that can be formatted and educationally managed in this or that way—with the added proviso that one's mind elements can be equally conditioned:

1) To realize or perceive certain kinds of information—which would equate to a condition of limited awareness. Meaning: To comprehend or acknowledge specific types of knowledge, which would indicate a state of restricted

consciousness; and

2) To NOT realize or perceive other kinds of information—which would equate to a condition of non-awareness or un-awareness. Meaning: to lack the realization or perception of other forms of information, resulting in a state of conditioned non-awareness or unawareness.

A profound question lingers: Why were the precise, crucial, straightforward, and vigorous definitions of AWARE deemed antiquated at one time, only to be replaced by convoluted and passive variations? And whose resilience can be molded through subtle influences and manipulation in such a manner?

As we contemplate the truly dreadful nature of this situation, it is important to consider the possibility there are states of unimpeded awareness. These states would not be influenced or controlled by external factors such as societal norms or motivations.

If we accept the existence of these unimpeded states, they could only truly be considered unimpeded if they were completely immune to outside influences.

Furthermore, for these states of awareness to become impeded, they must have existed in a pristine and untouched state beforehand.

In the realm of superpowers, it is essential to note that unimpeded awareness faculties must exist before their acquisition. Only then can they be shaped and influenced by societal norms and conditioning methods. The word "impede" carries a weighty significance in this context—to interfere with progress, to block potential, to hinder growth.

One cannot impede something that does not already exist in an unimpeded state. It is the very presence of this unbridled potential that allows for the shaping and molding of these extraordinary capacities. Without it, there would be nothing to impede in the first place.

It is within the realm of possibility to consider that if an individual's superpower faculties are not functioning or engaged, it could be due to hindrances in their auxiliary awareness spectrums—for a multitude of potential reasons. The main issue, though, with attempting to activate superpowers is that it's difficult to do so using passive awareness techniques.

In order to examine active and passive types of awareness, it is first necessary to make a slight detour into the meanings of the terms SYSTEM and AUTONOMY.

To organize is to bring together and arrange various elements, parts, or segments into a cohesive and functional unit. The concept of organization implies the existence of individual components that can be joined together to form a unified whole. Whether it is assembling disparate parts or shaping existing pieces, the ultimate goal remains the same: creating a functioning SYSTEM:

1) "A regularly interacting or interdependent group of items forming a unified whole";
2) "A group of interacting bodies [or phenomena] under the influence of related forces."

When considering the definitions above, it is important to acknowledge that individuals have their own personal experiences and understandings. In this too, it is likely they also possess a multitude of innate awarenesses and faculties that are currently inactive.

To truly grasp this concept, imagine an individual with only one faculty—it is absurd and an extreme oversimplification.

In reality, every person possesses a vast spectrum of visible faculties augmented by an even larger spectrum of invisible ones that remain dormant or suppressed. It is evident that each type of faculty requires specific types of awareness for support and development.

So why is awareness only defined in general terms? Why does it not take into account the varying degrees and types of active and inactive faculties within each individual? Surely, there must be a range, a spectrum, of active and inactive "units" of awareness that align with each specialized faculty.

It thus becomes possible to consider the real existence of arrays of awareness which assist and support arrays of faculties, and which in turn download into arrays of perceptions.

The labels and definitions become insignificant when compared to what one can truly perceive and understand. Whether it is called a superpower or not, the only thing that truly matters is one's awareness and understanding. Sequential arrays and multiple ranges are evident in everything, indicating a systemic nature. They are systems, made up of interconnected and interdependent items, parts, arrays or phenomena that come together to form a unified whole.

At this point, whether the parts, arrays, faculties, awarenesses are active, inactive, or desensitized now remains the only real point of interest regarding the superpowers.

The meanings of AUTONOMY, together with the meanings of the terms AWARENESS and SYSTEMS, altogether constitute one of the most fundamental concepts regarding the start-up of superpower functioning.

The definitions for AUTONOMY and AUTONOMOUS given in most dictionaries are:

1) The quality or state of being self-governed, especially as regards the right of self-government;
2) A self-governed state, nation, or country;
3) Having the right or power of self-government;
4) Undertaken or carried on without outside control;
5) Existing or capable of existing independently; and
6) Responding, reacting, evolving, or developing independently of the whole, as seen in growth, for example.

With these definitions in mind, it is commonly accepted that the term AUTONOMY refers to a self-governing nation, state, or country, or to an entity with complete independence. Just the same, in recent times, psychiatry and psychology have appropriated the term AUTONOMY for their own purposes. Thus, in the language of psychiatry specifically, AUTONOMY is defined as follows:

1) The quality or state of being self- governing. The living organism does not represent merely an inactive element but is, to a large extent, a self-governing entity.
2) The biological process, therefore, is not entirely a result of external forces, but is in part governed by specific biological forces which are endogenous.
3) The organism possesses a certain degree of freedom; i.e., it acts according to its own inherent

nature, which is based on intrinsic forces, and not under the compulsion of outside influences. (**Psychiatric Dictionary, 5th Edition**, Oxford University Press, 1981.)

It is obvious by now that I am attempting to attach the superpowers to categories of active autonomous awarenesses. But the overarching and overall situation remains somewhat more complicated—simply because passive awarenesses are of great importance and as such play a very large and vital role in formatting realities of the external worlds.

To better understand this concept, let us consider that our reliance heavily banks on receiving information from external sources.

This information is then passively absorbed and stored in our minds. Once these passive channels reach a certain level of significance, we use them to navigate our way through the world around us.

Taking actions like these is not just expected, but a crucial aspect of navigating external factors. In simpler terms, one's reality is shaped by and in relation to persuasive external influences. In this scenario, one's "ego" can become intertwined with the constant flow of outside forces.

These external factors, consequentially, are often reduced to limited understandings—and at times, even false notions—resulting in their faltering instability and impermanence.

As the external factors shift and evolve, those who have simply accepted and adapted to the previous reality are suddenly left behind. Their sense of self in relation to these external forces is now comparable to a kite whose string has been violently severed. They are adrift, untethered from the familiar and struggling to find their place in this new world around them.

In the realm of superpowers, extensive research in the fields of psychical research and parapsychology has uncovered a wealth of knowledge that serves as an external source for those who seek it.

This information is then absorbed into the passive awareness of individuals, where they construct their own unique understanding and beliefs about the parapsychological versions of these powers.

Along with this, there exists a specific vocabulary and terminology—para-speak—used to describe and identify these abilities within the realm of parapsychology.

In this sense, the parapsychology versions and their supposed knowledge contexts now act as external forces and influences that can be in-put or in-taken into the passive awarenesses of interested individuals—and even into the passive awareness layers of the disinterested and the antagonistic skeptics, scientists, philosophers, and whatnot.

Those that accomplish something along such lines can be said to be in close passive proximity to the information put forth from those versions of the superpowers. But alas! perhaps still quite distant from the more truly active, autonomous nature of the superpowers themselves.

To truly understand the difference between passive and active awareness, it is important to identify their key characteristics.

A clear distinction can be made by acknowledging passive awareness is non-volitional in nature. It relies on being receptive and open to external stimuli, as if welcoming them with open arms.

The process of receiving external information more or less requires a non-volitional-passive state of some kind. Without this state, the information will not register, imprint, or become formatted, leaving one unable to truly claim awareness of it.

In contemplating the relationship between volition and awareness, one must also consider the presence of power and its counterpart, powerlessness. If we can equate non-volition with passive awareness, then it follows that active awareness is tied to volition.

This idea suggests a connection between power and active awareness, as opposed to its distant relation with passive awareness.

It's plausible to surmise that power resides more comfortably in the realm of active awareness rather than passive, symbolizing strength and control over one's reality.

In martial arts, for example, different types of awareness are not only acknowledged, but crucial. In fact, there is a strong emphasis on distinguishing between passive and active awareness during training.

The key to developing quick reflexes that do not rely on conscious thought lies in utilizing intentional and volitional awareness.[8]

In any event, examples of active awarenesses are seldom seen because societal conditioning formats generally direct cognitive attention not toward, but away from them.

---

[8] Elizabeth Bergen Bartel, one of the University of West Georgia's 2022 Ingo Swann Fellowship recipients, centered her research on the psychological states of past sword masters and their relation to flow states, specifically relating to "the zone" and induced hyperconsciousness. A video of her lecture can be found within the Empiricist page of the website ingoswann.com.

LIKE A FISH IN WATER, THE LAST THING THE FISH WILL PROBABLY NOTICE IS THE WATER.

-- Ingo Swann, Psychic Literacy

PERCEPTION: DIRECT, INDIRECT, AND TACTILE

At their core, superpowers of the human bio-mind are all information-dealing faculties. Every aspect of the human bio-mind's abilities can be traced back to this fundamental function. Without these information-dealing faculties, none of the other attributes would exist. Therefore, if any of these superpower faculties are not being utilized, their associated attributes and extensions will also remain dormant.

Among these faculties is perception, an essential attribute of the information-dealing systems. It is not a primal or first instance of anything, but rather a crucial aspect that allows us to interact with and understand the world around us.

We frequently hear and use the term PERCEPTION, but do we truly comprehend its significance? People may nod along as if they grasp it, but do they really?

If you ASK a few people what it means, well, now occurs a pause, sometimes followed by: "Well, let's see ... (a hiatus of verbiage) ....". Sometimes someone will respond: "It means what I perceive, that's perception." Or: "It's what I see." Others might say: "OK. I guess I'd better look it up."

It is an undeniable truth that as a species, we possess the gift of perception—unless our senses are impaired, in which case we are rendered unable to see or comprehend certain things.

We must acknowledge that while perceptions can lead us to knowledge, they can also deceive us and hinder our understanding. For example, if we hold the belief that psychic abilities are rooted in perception, we may be blinded to the reality that this is not true.

In fact, all living organisms rely on some form of perceptual acuity for survival. It's impossible to imagine a creature without any sensory faculties surviving for long in this world. Just picture it—a lifeform devoid of perception, doomed to inevitable extinction.

In other words, PERCEPTION is so fundamental to our species that it is practically synonymous with FUNCTIONAL LIFE itself—and that life, or at least the living of it, becomes increasingly dysfunctional as the perceptual faculties themselves become—or are.

And since perception is so fundamental, we think that perception must be the answer to everything. This remains a convincing truism—until the question arises why we DO NOT perceive something when enough evidence is present to indicate that we should?

After considering all the aforementioned contexts, it becomes clear without perception, we are nothing. The very foundation upon which all other concepts are built is based on the concept of perception. Once one begins to understand and accept that there is more to perception than initially thought, however, it becomes apparent that perception is not just perception, but something entirely different. If our understanding of perception is not accurate, then a basic definition of it is insufficient.

Merely acknowledging that we have perceptions is not enough—in fact, it could be harmful. To truly awaken and activate our superpowers, we must have a deep understanding of the nature of perception.

The arduous process of researching and compiling all the knowledge and understanding surrounding perception has been a strenuous and grueling task. But through this research, one may stumble upon brief yet profound statements such as "You ARE your perceptions..." or "What you perceive, so shall you be...," leading to the realization that our perceptions shape us, and our lack of perceptions do not. The enduring saying "I think, therefore I am," does not quite capture the truth.

Thinking only occurs after perceiving; therefore, it is the quantity and quality of our perceptions that truly define us as an individual. But, and it is a big BUT, our systems can only interpret information that is allowed into them.

Beyond the confines of our five "known" senses lies a vast sensorium[9] waiting to be discovered. A realm filled with sights that go beyond the visible spectrum, sounds that surpass our perceived audible range, and sensations that extend far beyond the boundaries of touch. This world exists all around us, but is often blocked from entering our systems, preventing us from perceiving its existence at all.

For some clue of this sensorium perhaps we can turn to the ever-evolving world of science and research. There we can find new and ongoing discoveries that reveal the biological foundations of this extended level

---

[9] Derived from the Latin word sensus which means "the ability to perceive," sensorium refers to the supposed location of sensation and perception. In Late Latin, it is known as sensōrium, combining sentiō (to feel, perceive) with -ōrium (a suffix for a designated place or function).

of awareness.

This groundbreaking field can be best defined as PARABIOLOGY, surpassing traditional concepts of biology—alternatively, we could employ the expression PARAPSYCHOBIOLOGY, which we might call bio-communications or bio-information transfer.[10]

This emerging field explores the mind-body connection and how information is exchanged between living organisms on a cellular level. To provide a comprehensive understanding of the cutting-edge and highly technical disciplines at play, I will now list twenty of them for you:

1) Electro-chemical physiology;
2) Neurobiology;
3) Neuropsychology;
4) Bio-radiation studies;
5) Hormone and Hormonal transmission research;
6) Chemical signal research;
7) Bio-electric research;
8) Brainwave research;
9) Bio-sensitivity research;
10) Bio-electric information transfer research;
11) Sensory coding research;
12) Bio-magnetic navigation research;
13) Bio-electronic systems research;
14) Bio-electric field detection research;
15) Electrophysiological studies;

---

[10] In 1975, the CIA commissioned a report on Soviet literature that explored their progress in the field of psychotronics, the Eastern bloc's term for parapsychology. The report, titled **NOVEL BIOPHYSICAL INFORMATION TRANSFER MECHANISMS**, was published in 1976, and includes a bibliography of literature pertaining to this topic. This document can be found in the CIA reading room and on the website conjunction.world.

16) Pheromone and pheromone transfer research;
17) Multi-stability in perception research;
18) Subliminal perception research;
19) Neuro-magnetic response research; and
20) Bio-infrared and bio-ultraviolet perception research.

Each one explores specific aspects of human physiology and biological processes, from the chemical reactions within our bodies to the subtle electric signals that govern our thoughts and actions. These fields encompass a vast range of knowledge and techniques, all working towards a deeper understanding of the intricate workings of the human bio-mind and bio-body.

These recent breakthroughs in understanding the biological foundations of our faculties can be classified into five main categories. While it may seem technical, these broad categories include:

1) Microscopic chemical receptors and sensors;
2) Minute chemico-electro receptors and sensors;
3) Neural networks exchanging information within the body's internal bio-substrates;
4) Bio-electromagnetic receptors and sensors for gathering information; and
5) Bio-information transfer networks operating at the atomic, molecular, and neurological levels.

If the terminology of these new concepts seems daunting, there is no need to worry. They simply mean that we have surpassed the narrow understanding of relying solely on our five senses and have evolved to possess an abundance of exceptional abilities through delicate systems of receptors and sensors at the cellular, nervous, chemical, and bio-electromagnetic levels.

It can be best understood as every cell, perhaps even every atom, in our physical being serving as a receptor or sensor in some form. In essence, we are living and breathing arrays of exquisitely elegant and intricate receptors and sensors. All these receptors and sensors are actively gathering information—and potential knowledge.

In a broader sense, these intricate networks of receptors can integrate with our natural "five" senses. With adaptive learning, they can even fuse with our cognitive abilities, resulting in what has commonly been referred to as Psi faculties.

These incredible abilities allow us to tap into powers beyond our normal physical and mental capabilities, opening up a whole new world of possibilities and understanding.

At this point, I could adumbrate into a glut of scientific papers, over a thousand in fact, that have been published in esteemed periodicals such as **Nature**, **Scientific American**, and **Discover**, all documenting these groundbreaking discoveries. But the researchers behind these studies never dare to use terms like Psi, psychic abilities, or parapsychology. To do so would result in swift rejection from the publication. It seems the editors and peer-review systems are unaware that phrases like "bioinformation transfer over distance" are essentially synonymous with the para-speak terms of "telepathy," "clairvoyance," and "remote viewing."

Now transport yourself back to the year 1984 where a book, published by Simon & Schuster and written by Robert Rivlan and Karen Gravelle, awaits you. Its pages are filled with a comprehensive bibliography of scientific sources, yet it's very easy to read. The title, **Deciphering the Senses: The Expanding World of**

Human Perception, may seem somewhat deceptive at first glance. After all, the world of human perception is not physically expanding, but rather our understanding of it is slowly unraveling. In fact, a more fitting title for this enlightening read might have been something like **The Infinite Realm of Biological Understanding: Unveiling the Mysteries of PSI and Other Anomalous Perceptions**.

The revelations and findings compiled and shared within this book may be written in a style that appeals to the general public, but they are rooted in rigorous scientific discoveries achieved by researchers outside of the field of parapsychology.

These discoveries, independent from any influence or bias, provide compelling evidence for the existence of certain forms of Psi. They fulfill the long-standing scientific demand for a biological and organic basis for Psi phenomena.

The book's flyleaf boasts a bold statement: "For centuries we have used an oversimplified and inaccurate model to explain the human senses." The pages within reveal a deep exploration into the complexities of human perception.

High school biology classes may still teach the traditional "five senses," but according to recent scientific research, there are many more than just five. Authors Rivlan and Gravelle challenge readers to expand their understanding as they redefine the spectrum of human perceptions from the ordinary to the extraordinary.

With captivating language, chapter one lays out the foundation for seventeen senses beyond our usual five. The authors take great care in placing these newly discovered senses in the context of our familiar ones, unraveling the intricate web of sensory experiences that make up our daily lives. Eight chapters lay this groundwork, leading up to the highly anticipated ninth chapter titled "Extra-sensory perception."

Despite its groundbreaking content, the book was met with mixed reviews upon its release and is now out of print. For those, however, willing to seek it out, it offers a profound perspective on human perception that is well worth the effort.

Let's be clear here, the two authors are not discussing abstract concepts or theories of psychology or mental processes. They are delving into the physical realities within our biology—the intricate and delicate network of tiny physical-chemical bio electromagnetic "receptors" and "sensors" that function as information processing resources within our bio-bodies.

It is evident that relying solely on our five basic senses cannot fully account for the vast range of sensory experiences humans are capable of. Just consider how essential these additional senses are for survival—whether it be navigating treacherous seas, scaling towering mountains, competing in intense sports like football or basketball, exploring new territories, inventing revolutionary technologies, mastering martial arts, or seeking out intimate connections with others. The mention of "automatic reflexes" or "intuition" signals a shift beyond the realm of our basic five senses and into the realm of these additional and crucial senses.

The concept of seventeen new senses may seem overwhelming, but each one works in tandem with the others to create a comprehensive and intricate list. These sensations have often been categorized as "psychic," but recent research has shed more light on their true nature.

And so, let's take a closer look at some of these

extraordinary senses. For instance, the bio-body has a functioning vomeronasal system equipped with receptors that can detect minuscule amounts of chemical signals. This allows for subliminal reception of an individual's sexual receptivity, fear, anger, and other emotions—commonly referred to as "psychic vibe sensing."

In another category, scientists have developed a revolutionary tool called the SQUID, which measures and classifies the brain's electrical activity beyond just the scalp. This has led to groundbreaking discoveries about the extent of our bio-electric activity, including sensors not only in the skin but also in neuropeptides that transmit subtle sensory information through the immune system and into the brain. These transmissions ultimately extend back out into the bio-body and its surroundings, including its bio-electromagnetic field.

After centuries of speculation, and being housed in mysticism, the existence of bio-electromagnetic fields extending beyond the scalp and skin has finally been discovered. These ethereal energies, aptly referred to as "auras," have long been the subject of fascination for clairvoyants and spiritualists.

But now, thanks to authoritative scientific sources like Rivlan and Gravelle, we can confidently say that thoughts may truly have wings. The authors boldly hypothesize that individuals possess an innate faculty to sense these bio-electromagnetic fields, allowing them to read the thoughts of others from a distance. This heightened perception could explain the abilities of psychics and mystics who have long claimed to possess such powers.

And while this may seem far-fetched to some, it is a well-known belief among ancient civilizations and nomadic cultures, as well as those street-smart city dwellers in New York.

For over fifty years, researchers in the fields of electromagnetism and bio-electromagnetism have pondered the same question. It's important to note that extensive evidence of bio-electromagnetism was first presented towards the end of the previous century, yet it has largely been overlooked by both scientific psychology and parapsychology. These two fields have seemingly managed to completely ignore its existence altogether, despite its potential significance.

Have you ever considered the fact that in addition to being a physical, organic being with eyes, livers, hearts, and various appetites, you are also a bio-electronic entity? It's a fascinating thought to ponder. Dr. Robert O. Becker, one of the foremost researchers in the United States in the field of electromagnetism and bio-electromagnetism, certainly thinks so.

In 1985, he co-wrote a book called **The Body Electric: Electromagnetism and the Foundation of Life** (William Morrow, 1985) with Gary Selden. This book delves into the incredible story of our bioelectric selves and how they shape our existence. Another important book on this subject is Harold Saxton Burr's **Blueprint for Immortality: The Electric Patterns of Life** (Neville Spearman, 1973). It is interesting to note, despite being an American researcher, Burr struggled to find an American publisher for his groundbreaking work.

Bob Becker, a renowned expert in the field of bio-electromagnetism, has made numerous exceedingly bold statements regarding its implications for Psi phenomena.

In 1977, he published an article titled "An Application of Direct Current Neural Systems to Psychic Phenomena" in the journal **Psychoenergetic Systems** (Vol. 2, pp. 189-196). In it, he posited that "The concept of a primitive electronic communication system in all living things can be a powerful tool in understanding both 'normal' and 'paranormal' phenomena that have thus far eluded scientific explanation." Through his extensive research, he has shown that human beings are intimately connected to the universe through a complex web of electromagnetic energy.

At this point, I believe I've now presented for your consideration the rudiments of a Particular Situation. The Particular Situation consists of three factors: (1) science demanded that a bio-organic explanation for superpower faculties be found before it could accept them as real; (2) bio-organic explanations have been found for many kinds of superpower faculties; and (3) everyone seems to be ignoring both the facts and the implications of (2) as just stated.

As to more of what our additional senses are: Did you know the soles of your feet and palms of your hands contain minute magnetic receptors and sensors? These incredible components have the power to "recognize" even the smallest changes in local magnetism. This explains the ancient practice of dowsing as well as various forms of psychometry (the ability to perceive information about an object by simply holding it).

Be that as it may, these faculties are not easily harnessed. Only those who have trained their minds to tap into these receptors can truly experience their full potential. For those who haven't built strong neural pathways connecting these sensors to their cognitive faculties, these hidden powers may remain inaccessible and unknown.

The issue of nomenclature has long been a barrier between new discoveries and the more established concepts of psychical and parapsychological research.

This same barrier also hinders progress in the fields of enlightenment and transformation. To bridge this gap, let us examine some examples that highlight the differences between the two nomenclatures. These comparisons will shed light on how we can begin to unite the two and move forward in our understanding of these phenomena:

1) Receptors in the nose sensing systems that "smell" emotions, and that can identify motives, sexual receptivity, antagonism, benevolence, etc. (All these are formats of what are commonly referred to as psychic vibe sensing.)
2) Receptors in the ear sensing systems that detect and identify differences in pressure and electromagnetic frequencies (formats of ESP).
3) Skin receptors that detect balance and imbalance regarding what is external to the bio-body, even external at some astonishing distances (formats of remote-sensing, a mixed form of ESP and CLAIRVOYANCE).
4) Skin receptors that detect motion outside of the body, even when the body is asleep (a format of subliminal ESP).
5) Directional finding and locating receptors in the endocrine and neuropeptide systems (formats of DOWSING, intermixed with formats of cognitive ESP or INTUITION).
6) Whole-body receptors, including hair, that identify fluidic motions of horizontal, vertical, and diagonal, even if not visually perceived (as, for example, in the "psychic" portion of the martial art of Aikido).
7) Skin receptors that "recognize" the temperament of other biological organisms (a

format of Psi "reading").
8) Subliminal sensory systems which locate and identify pitch of sound, a sense of heat across great distances, a sense of frequencies and waves, either mechanical or energetic (all being formats of ESP and VIBE SENSING, sometimes also referred to as "shaman perceiving").
9) Receptors that identify positive and negative charged particles at the atomic level. (The term utilized for this in psychical research is "micro-psi," but which is rare. However, it has been convincingly demonstrated, especially in the case of C. W. Leadbeater who published **Occult Chemistry** (Theosophical Publishing House, 1908). Thirty years before the invention of the electron-microscope he correctly described sub-atomic particles, many undiscovered at the time, but discovered since. Micro-psi faculties are mentioned as one of the ancient Siddhis of ancient India (see, for example, Yoga Sutras of Patanjali).
10) Microsystem transducing of various forms of mechanical, chemical, and electromagnetic energy into meaningful nerve impulses (all commonly thought of as FORMS OF ESP).
11) Receptors that sense gravitational changes (a form of PSYCHIC DOWSING).
12) Neurological senses for interpreting modulated electronic information by converting it into analog signals for mental storage, interpretation, and cognition (one of the human bio-mind bases for TELEPATHY).
13) Bio-electronic receptors for sensing radiation, including X-rays, cosmic rays, infrared radiation, and ultraviolet light, all these receptors being

found in the retina of the eye (part of the basis for various forms of CLAIRVOYANCE).
14) Receptors that respond to exterior electrical fields and systems (producing forms of CLAIRVOYANCE and AURA "READING").

Today, the following highly specialized sensing systems are referred to in the new sciences as HUMAN SEMAPHORE CAPACITIES.

15) Skin receptors for sensing perceptions of bonding or antagonism (thought of as forms of INTUITION).
16) Senses for non-verbal "language" communicating (thought of as a form of TELEPATHY or VIBE SENSING).
17) Combined sensing systems (neural networks) for making meaning out of at least one hundred thirty identified nonverbal physical gestures and twenty basic kinds of nonverbal messages (thought of as INTUITIONAL CHARACTER ASSESSMENT or a particular form of CLAIRVOYANCE).
18) Receptors that trigger alarm and apprehension before their sources are directly perceived (a particularly valuable type of PSYCHIC FORESIGHT, FORESEEING, INTUITION).
19) Sensing systems for registering and identifying nonverbal emotional waves (a form of INTUITION and/or TELEPATHY or CLAIRVOYANCE).

The following are now known to be associated with the PINEAL GLAND if it is healthy and in good working order.

20) Senses and memory-stores cycles of light and darkness, anticipating them with accuracy as the daily motions of the sun and moon change (a kind of PSYCHIC FORECASTING or FUTURE SEEING).
21) Senses and responds to solar and lunar rhythms, solar disruptions (flares, sunspots) and moon-caused tidal changes (water or geophysical ones) and can sense "coming" earthquakes and storms (a form of PREDICTIVE ESP especially noted in sailors, farmers, but also in cows, dogs, cats, and snakes).
22) If the pineal gland is fully functional, it acts as a nonvisual photo-receptor (the psychic equivalent being "X-RAY VISION").

As we explore the various senses and sensing systems, it becomes apparent that there are even more intricacies at play. Some of these systems may seem like ones we have already discussed, but they actually function on a completely different basis.

It is now believed that this basis is centered around WATER—a vital component of our bio-body, nerve systems, and even our physical brain. The mystery lies in how exactly water is used to create such a complex network of interconnected sensing systems.

One theory suggests the vibrations of water molecules act as radar or sonar antennae, linking throughout the bio-body and forming an incredibly fluid system of detection. These "liquid antenna" systems appear to detect specific categories, almost like individualized and refined senses. In the past, these categories have been dismissed as "psychic," "ESP," "clairvoyant," or "intuitive"—deemed impossible to explain.

23) Sense of non-visual wave motions.
24) Sense of non-visual oscillating patterns.
25) Sense of magnetic fields.
26) Sense of infrared radiation.
27) Sense of electrical energy.
28) Sense receptors for local AND distant sources of heat. (This is an unnamed PSI faculty, but one familiar to Amerindians.)
29) Sense of geo-electromagnetic pulses, magnetic fields, especially biological ones (psychic equivalents unidentified and unnamed).
30) Although the mechanisms are not at all understood, the liquidic sensing detectors apparently are somehow involved in the remote-sensing of anything at a distance, however great. The results, of course, are remote viewing, remote hearing, remote tasting, and so forth.

In the vast expanse of the bio-body, countless sensory receptors are spread throughout, relaying information to the mind-body interface—if such a term can accurately describe it.

Millions of whole-body receptors are dedicated to detecting pheromones, sexual receptivity, fear, love, admiration, danger, pain in others, and even intentions. These were once considered inexplicable forms of ESP or so-called VIBE SENSING and PSYCHIC "READING" but are now being recognized as integral parts of our sensory systems. It's important to note this list is far from complete and is constantly expanding as we gain a deeper understanding of ourselves.

Along those lines, among the many technical books available, one stands out as particularly approachable and informative: **Sensation and Perception: An Integrated Approach** by H.R. Schiffman, published by John Wiley & Sons in 1976. Despite its age, this book remains a valuable resource and contains an extensive bibliography of sources. This is in addition to the previously noted **Deciphering the Senses: The Expanding World of Human Perception** by Robert Rivlan and Karen Gravelle.

Its first chapter delves into the fascinating topic of SEVENTEEN SENSES, providing readers with a thorough analysis and a comprehensive bibliography that builds upon the one found in Schiffman's book. It is interesting to note that despite the availability of these and other enlightening works, they were largely disregarded and the belief in only five physical senses continues to prevail even today. One could surmise that perhaps these books were overlooked because they encouraged people to explore their extended sensory systems and uncover their full potential.

As we contemplate our perceptions, we may unconsciously draw a line between ourselves and the senses that guide us. Except, if we truly observe, we will come to realize that we do not merely possess these senses—we are these senses. They are intricately woven into our being, guiding us through each moment of our existence. Our senses are the gateway through which we experience the world around us, merging with our consciousness in a dance of ever-changing sensations. As we fully embrace this realization, we will begin to see the beauty and interconnectedness of all that surrounds us.

In this way too, one of the most daunting obstacles to overcome is the widely held belief there is a direct link between the perceiver and the object being perceived. This idea can often be heard in everyday conversations, as people will confidently state, "I had a direct perception of it, so I know what I saw."

It is understandable that this concept has been adopted, as it is a common cultural belief in the modern Western world. Irrespective, there is a lack of effort put into challenging or correcting this concept, especially when discussing it openly. The idea of "direct" perception in English can be traced back through time, but its origins are murky and difficult to pinpoint.

Despite this, many modern definitions do not explicitly state that perception is direct. It is often implied, assumed, or taken for granted. For example, the original 1828 **Noah Webster's** gives for TO PERCEIVE: "To have knowledge or receive impressions of external objects through the medium or instrumentality of the senses or bodily organs. To know: to understand: to observe. To be effected by; to receive impressions from [something]." All of which, of course, are referred to as PERCEPTION(S)—but without any reference as to how the perceptions come about.

In the face of the mounting evidence and knowledge that has surfaced since 1828, the concept of perception in the English language remains largely unchanged, stoically resistant to criticism or improvement.

Merely observing or receiving impressions is not enough to claim true understanding and knowledge. According to the dictionary, PERCEPTION is defined as an attainment of awareness or understanding, while TO PERCEIVE is simply becoming aware through the senses. But these definitions fail to capture the complexity of perception.

One may hear others speak of someone possessing "piercing perceptions," while simultaneously warning against being "a victim of one's own perceptions." And yet, can there truly be a victim when it comes to something as subjective as perception? Awareness and understanding are often conflated, but they are truly separate entities—one can be aware of something without understanding it at all or understand something without any prior awareness.

As such, the concept of perception can be a confusing one, often leaving us unsure of what we truly understand. Whether we actively seek out and discover or passively take-in information, both processes suggest a direct connection between the perceiver and the perceived.

The active format involves a determined search, discovery, and piercing, while the passive format allows for a more relaxed receiving. These two formats do imply, however, a direct link between the individual and their surroundings.

Yet, despite these two options being widely accepted, there may in fact be three types of perception states: (1) passive in-take; (2) active outward seeking; and (3) not much of either. And if the existence of the third type above is admitted and plotted on the standard Bell curve, it might turn out that most experiences are made up of this type. You see, having perceptions either of type (1) or (2) might mean that one perceives too much, or perceives what others do not. And in either case, one would tend to depart from the "normal."

In this sense, there may exist at least two distinct types of superpower faculties that operate in different ways: (1) the passive PERCAPERE (to take thoroughly) type in which the experiencer simply absorbs perceptions without exerting any influence (this type would entail a one-way flow into the individual); and (2) the active PERCEANT (piercing, penetrating) type in which the experiencer actively penetrates and acutely gathers perceptions, followed by a return pathway through which the gathered information is processed.

These two types may function separately or in conjunction with each other, contributing to the overall perceptual experience of an individual.

It is worth pointing up that our prevailing conceptual reality is constructed upon the unremitting influx and interpretation of perceptions. This becomes particularly evident in individuals who seek out "psychic" tutelage, as they naturally anticipate an enhancement of their passive in-flow perceptions. It is almost as if they are expecting to be immersed in a flood of new sensory experiences.

And indeed, this is exactly what happens when one reads a book on how to become more psychic—they unconsciously expect to be exposed to information about receiving perceptions. It is also important to note that those who claim to receive information or images through their psychic abilities must possess a highly developed passive PERCAPERE perception system. For them to excel in their craft, their perceptual systems must be finely tuned to the passive receiving aspect of perceiving. Because, after all, they have mastered the art of receiving perceptions and translating them into meaningful messages.

But, if such a person were tasked with locating a missing person or a hidden dead body, they would need to rely on the active out-going PERCEANT type of perception—the penetrating, searching and keenly-finding ability. Functional examples of this type seem a rarity, and which may be why not many have emerged to aid law enforcement activities. Some do exist, in spite of that.

In any event, one can now see the incredible

complexity of perception. It is not just a singular concept, but rather a collection of various types and forms. There are at least two distinct kinds present, with even more waiting to be discovered. This realization brings an important distinction into focus within the broad concept of perception: how and in what manner each individual perception comes about or is formed.

Clearly, perceptions do not simply materialize out of thin air and cease to exist. Numerous functions and intricate processes are at play, shaping the very essence of what we perceive. These details, though, are often overlooked or misunderstood in our general understanding of perception.

The predominant collective belief is that perception is akin to seeing through the eyes, a concept that harkens back to outdated notions about the mechanics of vision.

There is a pervasive belief that the eye simply captures images of the objects it gazes upon. But in truth, the eye is a complex and intricate creation made up of tiny structures called rods and cones. These photosensors are exquisitely sensitive to light and work together as a team to create an elaborate system for detecting and interpreting light, known as "interference patterns." Each interaction between objects and light produces a unique pattern, almost like a visual language that our eyes translate into understanding.

But this is just the beginning. The process then moves on to a series of steps where the incoming bits of information are sent to be stored in our memory. These bits are compared to existing bits already stored there, searching for a match or similarity. This continues until a compatible match is found, triggering what we know as "recognition." It's almost like building a hologram, where all the compatible bits from memory storage come together to reconstruct or fabricate an image—what we call a "mental image picture." In this enigma lies a crucial missing piece: where do the reconstructed holograms originate from, and why do they form? The answers to these questions remain unknown.

One thing that is known for certain, however, is that everything we perceive—absolutely everything—is simply "information" that has been reconfigured into formats recognizable only through our memory storage. So, when an individual claims to receive impressions or images, they are not actually receiving anything of the sort.

They may indeed be receiving "signals," but these signals are merely being used to reconstruct familiar patterns and images stored in our memories. If there is only a partial match between the incoming signals and those stored in our memory, then an "impression" is formed. If the matches fit seamlessly together, then a fully formed perception or thought emerges. And if there are no matches at all, then the incoming information simply remains undetected, invisible to our conscious awareness.[11]

The word capturing the essence of this concept is RECOGNIZE. It is worth noting that "recognize" holds a deeper meaning: to RE cognize, or to RE formulate something in the mind. This leads us to a fitting definition of perception—a reconstructed image that is recognizable and can be comprehended.

A perception is a re-cognizable formulation born from very carefully piecing and placing together information, but this re-construction is only possible

---

[11] The only exception to this rule seems to be intuition, which is often described as a gut feeling rather than a concrete perception.

based on an individual's personal memory storage, unique to them and no one else. Ultimately, the concept of "perceptions" is a construct and does not exist as a tangible entity. What does exist are the interpretations and reconstructions of information within our minds, which we then label as perceptions. But the truth is that perception encompasses a multitude of intricate components, beyond just sight alone.

In spite of its complexity, the concepts mentioned above have not been widely accepted in mainstream society. The idea that every perception is not directly experienced, but rather a reconstructed version created by the mind, has been scientifically recognized for quite some time. Even well-respected scientific intellectuals and philosophers were aware of this truth in the years leading up to the turn of the twentieth century.

As this understanding took root, it gave rise to mysterious maxims: "One's perceptions are not to be trusted" and "Don't put too much faith in your own or anyone's perceptions," among others. These maxims were, and still are, challenged by more fundamental consensus realities that ask the question: "If we can't trust our perceptions, then what can we trust?"

Apart from this challenge, commonly accepted consensus realities continue to operate based on receiving and trusting perceptions. This persists because these realities encompass the majority, and even unsuspecting subgroups, making it difficult to break away from their influence.

The evidence is undeniably strong when it comes to two crucial factors that are always at play: (1) What resides within the mind's vast stockpile of memories is often a comprehensive "dictionary of possibilities" or "slide library," inextricably linked not with one's mental capabilities, but rather with one's fundamental grasp of language. As a little-known French philosopher and keen observer of perception aptly states: "... it is from an electrical pattern taken from this individual slide-library that, with only minor adjustments, eventually materializes in your 'mind's eye.'" (2) On the other hand, what doesn't exist within this memory library is quite often devoid of any linguistic nomenclature, thus rendering it invisible to our conscious awareness.

Our supply of nomenclature is established and maintained by the collective realities that govern us—save for instances of "street-talk" and trendy yet unofficial ways of labeling something. Take for instance, "vibe sensing" and "psych out"; these two colloquial terms represent entirely valid potentials, but the general populace rarely acknowledges their end results also consist only of reconstructions, rather than direct perceptions.

To get straight to the point, in English we have a word for a specific animal—a camel. And in our minds, we have two distinct images stored in our memory library of this creature. So, when we encounter one or hear it mentioned, one of these electrical patterns will appear in our mind's eye. The first image is of a typical camel, with its distinctive humps and features. But there is also a second, less official image that may come to mind—that of the act of "humping," which can mean different things to different people but is associated with camels due to their name and behavior.

But, for Bedouins, seeing or hearing about a camel can trigger a multitude of different mental images. This reflects their cultural reality where there are various Arabic words for different types of camels based on their age, size, sex, spitting habits, temperament, use of their droppings, and even types of stubbornness. In English-speaking realities, a camel remains simply a camel, except within certain scientific fields that map the distinctions between different types of camels.

Looking back on everything previously mentioned, perception is not simply a singular experience, rather the culmination of countless non-conscious processes that in the end give rise to what we recognize as "perception."

This process is not a direct one, but rather a reconstruction made possible by one crucial factor: memory comparisons. And ultimately, the method for controlling and organizing our memories centers around effectively processing and transferring information which then produces thing-images.

As humans, we tend to view the world in terms of tangible objects and their physical attributes such as shape, size, and color. These things are given meaning and referred to as "it." We also think about the spatial relationships between these objects, how they are arranged in relation to each other. If we think of subjects or topics, we do so by first converting them into an IT-THING: for example, consider biology. IT is a science.

At the very core of most agreed upon realities lies IT-THINGS, and the primary terminology used is designed specifically to identify these IT-things. Even philosophical abstractions are considered IT-things, as they too serve as a means for understanding the world. This was especially true for organized psychical research groups that emerged in the 1880s, whose objective was to witness, examine, differentiate, and categorize what would later be known as "paranormal" phenomena.

To begin this process, each phenomenon had to be given a distinct identifier, transforming them into IT-THINGS. Examples included "IT is clairvoyance," "IT is levitation," "IT is mediumship," "IT is thought-transference,"—later replaced by the term-concept "telepathy"—and ultimately "IT is psychic."

In this way, the ideas of perception are inextricably bound to the concept of IT-THINGS. What we perceive is not necessarily a true reflection of the object itself, but rather a very defined reconstruction within our minds. Our perceptions act as filters, allowing us to identify and distinguish among THINGS before they manifest in our conscious awareness as reconstructed images.

Within the intricate web of human consciousness, there exists a mental framework known as basic IT-THINK. This mode of thinking allows us to navigate and survive in our world with an approximate success rate of ninety percent—unless, of course, there are gaps or holes within this framework.

These flaws can sometimes be corrected within the confines of our collective understanding of reality, where perception that aligns with consensus is deemed proper and successful, while anything outside of this norm is considered aberrant or undesirable.

But just beyond the boundaries of our all-encompassing IT-THINK lies a slightly different format of thought. This level explores the complexities of relationships between IT-things—objects, ideas, entities—rather than simply their individual properties.

Deciphering these relationships, however, is no easy task, as they must often be construed through observation and deduction. This higher level of thinking requires a deeper understanding and awareness of the connections and interplay between the IT-things that make up our world. The relationships between objects, known as IT-THINGS, can be divided into two categories: explicit and implicit.

The former are easily identifiable through logical reasoning, while the latter require a keen eye to detect due to the lack of objective cues. Thus, the detection of these implicit relationships often eludes deductive processes, except for those who possess a special ability to observe them.[12] And so there is a constant sharing of both explicit and implicit considerations. These thoughts and theories, this INFORMATION, shape our present general consensus realities. But what if this concept of consensus reality is not comprehensive enough? What if there exists a "gaping hole" in its interconnecting line-up of ideas, one that is invisible but crucially important to understanding our world? It may be overlooked because the seemingly complete and logical picture presented appears sufficient, but what hidden truths could be revealed by acknowledging this gap?

In terms of INFORMATION, when we think of something formed, we tend to think in terms of FORM only, not that something has PUT whatever it is INTO form or format. I now caution each who chances to read the above to slow down, focus a little, and notice two important factors: (1) that there is a vast and very incompatible raw difference between messages and the structure and shape of something; and (2) when we think of form as form, we tend to think of it as an IT object or subject, not as something which has been brought into or put into form by various shape-making, structure-making processes of some kind. In other words, something which is formed or has achieved form is the RESULT of whatever has caused it to take on

---

[12] These individuals are often labeled as intuitives. Ingo considered the deduction of implicit relationships as the fundamental and most widely shared form of intuition among all its other types. And here lies, Ingo said, a crucial hint for strengthening one's intuition—by first sharpening their deductive abilities in identifying implicit relationships.

shape-structure.

When it comes to the English language, the concept of "into form" seems to have been discarded or forgotten. We no longer consider how or why something takes on a certain form. This is a common tendency in English nomenclature, where end products are often seen as standalone objects rather than the result of processes—specifically, structural processes that are necessary for any form to be created. The best way to understand this is not through words, but through a visual diagram. One can easily create their own by mapping out the process of how an object obtains its form.

When we think of clairvoyance and its associated superpower faculties, we often imagine the images that a clairvoyant "sees" as the manifestation of this ability. We believe they possess a unique vision others do not, and that their means of seeing is beyond our grasp—hence the concept of clairvoyance. But in doing so, we overlook the fact that the true essence of clairvoyance lies not in what is seen, but rather in the informative processes that allow for such visions.

These form-making procedures always precede and shape the resulting images. In other words, if clairvoyance exists, it is the active IN + FORM processes that give rise to it, and not the other way around. Without these processes in motion, the clairvoyant would not be able to see anything at all.

When it comes to information, we often associate it with things we can hear or see in a tangible form, like text or images. This is because our understanding of information is heavily influenced by societal norms and beliefs, and we have successfully replicated this concept. The true nature of information, though, goes beyond its physical manifestation. By the time it reaches a spoken, printed, or visual form, it has already undergone a series of organizing processes.

Albeit the end-product still serves as a source of information we attempt to replicate and comprehend within our own minds. The word "duplicate" suggests reproducing or copying this information into our own heads, with the goal of understanding it.

In this sense, the information we in-put into our minds is conveyed through spoken, written, or visual formats. Although, even after the initial in-put, the process of conveying the information continues as it is filtered through our mental processing grids—extensions of our memory libraries mentioned earlier. If there are matches found between the new information and what already exists in our memory library, then a form of duplication occurs—known as "understanding." If no matches are found in the memory library, then the flow of information will be rerouted through the nearest similarity.

This diversion takes us a step further away from a complete understanding. And if no similarities can be found, then the recipient of this in-put will be left with an empty space, a void where knowledge should have been. The mind will struggle to make sense of the information and may ultimately "draw a blank."

In other words, INFORMATION is what we understand, even if only in a partial way. If the in-put does not result in "understanding," then it is NOT information.

The idea that I have just elucidated is often called ordinary perception, but to me, it is known as indirect perception. But there exists a type of perception that surpasses the boundaries of our well-defined perceptual and processing abilities and allows for access and comprehension of knowledge from sources beyond the realm of ordinary or indirect perception. It is known as direct perception, an elevated state of awareness achieved through its own processes.

For example, let's draw an analogy of a person having a dream. The person often remembers the dream visually, but their eyes were closed, and they were asleep, so their "seeing" in the dream was not with their eyes. So, this means that there must be a component of the human personality which has a capacity for direct perception of other levels of awareness which yields the same result as ocular vision, but which has nothing to do with the eyes.

The interconnected universe of direct perception holds much untapped potential and understanding. These processes operate with their own rules and logic, capable of perceiving and conveying information without the interference of consciousness. We often try to fit our perception into a singular reality that we believe is the only one.

Our consciousness is accustomed to viewing physical realities through our senses. This limited perspective has become our only sense of reality. Other parts of our mind, such as the unconscious or supraconscious, have been disregarded as having any true reality and are seen as subjective constructs that depend on our conscious perceptions.

This idea needs to be rejected for us to fully understand these deeper aspects of ourselves. To truly tap into these faculties, we must become aware of this aspect of ourselves and locate the buried processes at work. By applying focus to how these internal mechanisms function, we can begin to take control of our powers.[13]

---

[13] This is the basis for Ingo's book, **Everybody's Guide to Natural ESP**.

**TO FIND SOMETHING,
ONE NEEDS TO FOLLOW THE VIBES TO IT.**

-- Ingo Swann, Waking Dream Files

PERORATION

The concepts of awareness and perception are often linked with consciousness. Still, it is difficult to connect the "extra-ordinary" capabilities often attributed to consciousness with awareness and perception because they often reveal things we were not previously aware of.

In addition, there is another crucial obstacle in understanding consciousness. This lies in the modern notion that the brain is the sole source of our consciousness, sensory perceptions, and all other forms of awareness. This belief is deeply rooted in the modern worldview. It is also closely intertwined with another key concept—the idea that the physical brain cannot directly perceive or sense anything beyond the limits of our physical senses. For instance, the future cannot be sensed by the brain since it has not yet come into existence.

But then again, this contradicts what intuition does—it seems to have a direct line to perceiving the future, whether through subtle feelings or vivid mental images projected onto the mind's eye.

Therefore, you can see the challenge in attributing

all sensory experiences solely to the brain—which science has yet to pinpoint as the actual location of consciousness.

This concept bears a close relationship to another, older idea, often referred to as "externalization of the sensibilities." Here it's exceedingly important to note that "sensibilities" should not be confused with the senses.

While SENSIBLE refers to things that can be sensed, SENSIBILITY refers to a unique susceptibility to pleasurable or painful impressions, such as empathy or emotiveness. In simpler terms, a "sense" relates to direct sensory data while a "sensibility" is about experiencing these sensations and processing them emotionally.

Now, for the sake of speculation, one could argue that through physical touch and sensory in-put, we are able to gather IMPRESSIONS of all things in our surroundings.

In fact, the use of the word "representative" suggests just that—that we are receiving impressions rather than the actual objects themselves.

If we were to rephrase "the representation of everything" into "the representation information of everything," then it becomes apparent that there may exist what was once hypothesized but has since been forgotten during our modern times an extensive "sense organ."[14]

---

[14] Conceptualized by the ancient Greeks and Romans. For centuries, it has been acknowledged that the world as perceived by ancient Greeks and Romans was vastly different from our own. Their senses were attuned to patterns and processes of perception that are foreign to us in the modern era. They possessed a deep understanding of the intricate relationship between perception, knowledge, and understanding, a concept that we have only begun to scratch the surface of today.

So, if there is indeed a connection between sensory in-put and the impressions it creates, then it can be said that this process ultimately involves representations of everything around us. And because much of "everything" exists outside of our physical bodies, this conjunction or connectiveness must occur externally as well.

In terms of awareness and perception this representation of information means there is a transmission of information taking place. This transfer occurs when significant information from beyond the scope of one's normal cognitive abilities is somehow acquired and integrated into their consciousness.

This is most evident in cases of intuition or foreseeing future events, where information that was previously unknown to the individual suddenly becomes accessible to them.

The specific process by which this transfer takes place remains a mystery, but after examining many confirmed instances of these experiences, it can be said that the strength of the transfer can range from subtle to powerful—sometimes even overwhelmingly so. In these cases, the power of the experience is not only overwhelming for the individual's cognitive functions but can also affect THE MOTOR FUNCTIONS OF THE BIO-BODY ITSELF.

This can be seen in moments when a person suddenly and without explanution takes a step back from an impending mortal danger, without even being consciously aware of the danger's existence. If the person had relied on their rational mind to detect and process the danger, it likely would have been too slow to act and the danger would have struck before any understanding could be reached.

This compelling type of intuitive experience is

marked by a sudden suspension of cognitive and motor functions, as if something else has taken control. In these moments, the bio-body seems to be temporarily commandeered by a faster, more primal force that acts quickly to move it out of harm's way before the slower rational mind has even processed the danger.

In this type of experience, the transfer of information bypasses the ingrained reasoning functions completely and is directly transmitted to the automatic bio-motor response systems. During this process, the individual's cerebral functions are suspended or rendered blank.

The result is a lack of intellectual understanding about what occurred and how it happened—only a sense of knowing that it did happen after the fact of its occurrence. In these moments, the conscious mind plays no role; instead, something else takes over the bio-body's motor functions with lightning-like speed.

Therefore, there must also exist a mechanism capable of suspending cognitive function and seizing control of the bio-body's automatic response systems. In this way, it's almost comical to imagine how the mind and its cognitive processes must suspend themselves for this split-second intuition to occur.

In any event, it is understood world-wide that all the identifiable kinds of intuition involve matters outside, even alien to, the usual processes of both mind and consciousness functioning. Thus, it is fair to assume that we are not dealing with mind and consciousness processes, in that these cannot be seen to be the source of intuitive experiencing. I make this argument because first those processes are excruciatingly sluggish.

What is even more important to note, therefore, is that intuitive episodes impart knowledge not previously contained within one's standard conscious thought processes (also referred to as "mental information processing grids"). Indeed, mind and consciousness functioning seem to be incorporated WITHIN the "something" which induces intuitive experiencing.

This indescribable "something" must surpass the limitations of the mind, consciousness, and motor functions combined for such intuitive experiences to occur.

PLEASE BE AWARE HERE that the preceding discussion presents a thought-provoking new perspective. The conventional belief suggests that intuition—and other types of superpowers—stem from something within the mind or consciousness. I am proposing instead a reversal of this idea—that the mind-consciousness exists outside of this internal realm, separate from whatever may account for intuition and the other superpowers.

As I investigated intuition, one of the oldest and most widely experienced of all the superpowers, I became determined to find a concept that encompassed it. Although, after several years of searching, I was unable to find a fitting term that met each of the criteria.

During this time, I also began to recognize the limitations of the English language when it came to naming these types of superpowers. And it dawned on me that without a true proper understanding and conceptuulization, we cannot hope to have control over our own potential. If our understanding falls short in achieving control, then it is clear that we have not truly grasped what is necessary for mastery.

The significance of proper naming cannot be emphasized enough in this context. Not only does it facilitate communication with others, but it also serves as a crucial instrument for organizing and processing thoughts within our own minds. Without proper labels and terms for things we could potentially think about, those thoughts may never cross our minds. Nomenclature acts as a bridge between ideas and language, as one triggers the other in a continuous cycle. To have a rich and precise vocabulary is to have a vast landscape of concepts at our disposal, waiting to be explored through words and expressions. It is the foundation of critical thinking and expands the boundaries of our intellectual abilities.

In my search for an appropriate concept regarding the "something" which might conceptually incorporate the concepts of intuition, I had of course run across the term SENSORIAL.

This term is in most modern dictionaries. But it is so seldom used that hardly anyone is aware of its existence even in psychology or psychiatry—and in parapsychology as well where I have never seen or heard it utilized. Most modern dictionaries indicate that SENSORIAL is derived from the Latin SENSORIAL, the ancient meaning of which, so most American dictionaries state, was "sense organ."

Our complex human bio-bodies possess a multitude of senses, making it challenging for me to ponder what exactly a "sense organ" could be in the singular form.

As noted in a previous footnote, however, there is reason to believe that the term did not carry the same meaning during ancient times. In any case, modern English defines it as "the intricate parts of our brain responsible for receiving and deciphering sensory information; in essence, our entire sensory system."

A somewhat more extensive, and slightly more confusing, description of sensorial is found in the **Psychiatric Dictionary**. This description is worth quoting.

> **SENSORIAL:** The hypothetical seat of sensation or 'sense center' located in the brain, is usually contrasted with the MOTORIUM, the two constituting the so-called animal organ-system, while the nutritive and reproductive apparatus make up the vegetative organ-system. Occasionally this term is applied to the entire sensory apparatus of the bio-body.
>
> When a person is clearly aware of the nature of his surroundings, his sensorial is said to be 'clear' or 'intact.' For example, correct orientation is a manifestation of a clear sensorial.
>
> When a person is unclear, from a sensory (not delusional) standpoint, his sensorial is described as impaired or 'cloudy.' [SENSORIAL is used interchangeably with (organic) CONSCIOUSNESS.]
>
> The sensorial may appear to be disordered, when the psyche is intensely active, as it is in severe manic states, or when the patient is completely out of the environment, as he may be while in a phase of depressive stupor.

If you are struggling to understand the definition mentioned above, do not fret—because even the definition itself is full of uncertainties and complexities, as we will discuss further on. In any case, the definition introduces us to a term known as "motorium," so it is important for us to have some understanding of what it refers to.

According to the provided explanation, motorium can be defined as "(1) The area of the brain responsible for motor function; and (2) The faculty of the mind that governs volition (similar to how perception is governed by the sensorial and thinking by the intellect)." It may be worth noting there seems to be some confusion surrounding this term: while it is believed to refer to a specific area of the brain, it is also described as a mental faculty associated with volition. This faculty is set apart from the functions of the sensorial, which include perception, intellect, and thinking.

After careful examination of these definitions, a clear distinction between sensorial and motorium arises, particularly in the context of modernist thinking. Yet, this supposed distinction poses a significant problem. It can be easily demonstrated that perception, intellect, and thinking themselves are all volitional processes. To further clarify, many terms beginning with VOLA or VOLI denote some form of motion. In fact, our English word for volition is derived from the same French word which translates to "will."

Both these words can trace their origins back to the Latin term VOLANT, meaning "flying, rapid movement, unceasing motion, or constant fluttering." This description aptly captures the essence of our perceptions, intellect, and thinking processes—and possibly even the sensorial experience as a whole.

The concept of distinguishing between sensorial, motorium, perception, and thinking can be confusing because all these systems involve some form of motion. But when it comes to intuition or future-seeing, the movement is in the transfer—or attempted transfer—of information from an unknown source to the cognitive intellect. Without established concept grids that are relevant to this information, the chances are slim for the cognitive intellect to perceive it.

Moving expeditiously along then, we are now obliged to note American dictionaries stipulate that SENSORIAL is taken from the same word in Latin. Although, the reputable **OXFORD DICTIONARY** reveals that the Latin term was derived from the root verb SENTIRE—meaning "to feel."

Finally, we come across a concept that aligns with intuitive experiences. They often begin with a feeling, and in many cases, that is all there is to it—a sensation. "I had a gut feeling." "I felt a hunch." A strong sense that something has or will happen, an inner knowing of right or wrong, a warning of sorts.

If mental image pictures accompany the intuitive experience—as well as other superpowers—it is quite credible that they were stimulated into existence because of what was felt. In any event, it is unthinkable that the mental image pictures could come first—that we then examined them for the feelings incorporated in them—and then, from that examination, derived the intuition, and then the gut-feelings and hunches. This would be "doing" intuition backward, for the non-imaging feelings almost always come first.

In this case, the concept of the SENSORIAL is a perfectly good candidate for consideration when it comes to the superpowers of the human bio-mind. It is redolent with the externalization of sensibilities idea and serves to switch focus from internal biomechanisms to external factors. It is quite holistic—in that it would seem to include not only the bio-body but its energy fields, and which energy fields are certainly linked to the sensory receptor arrays of the bio-mind organism.

And indeed, in my personal experience and research, the switching of focus from brain or mind or body to the sensorial seems to permit conduits of so-called "extra-sensory" information to begin taking place.

But the conjunction would have to take place at a certain location—and so without doubt we might be referring to the fields or "auras" which surround the bio-body proper. Such fields or auras are referred to as energy bodies to distinguish them from the physical aspects of the bio-body.

If this were to be the case, then the SENSORIAL, functioning as the ultimate "sense organ," would encompass not only the physical components of the bio-mind but also its energy fields, possibly even those of an electronic nature.

Essentially, the "anatomy" of the SENSORIAL goes beyond just the tangible elements of the bio-body and extends to all aspects of its energy, with the potential exception of the conscious mind which often operates within the confines of its own mental processing grids.

And if we accept that "everything" includes past, present, and future, then the "representations of everything" would inevitably incorporate all three as well.

The manifestation of emotions and perceptions,

as distinct from internal senses, is undoubtedly intertwined with the majority of superpowers. And if we accept this premise, then it is but a mere leap to consider the sensorial realm as the "vehicle" from which representations are derived.

Though, it remains a perplexing concept to fathom how these impressions actually "arrive," unless there is some mechanism in place (1) to link them back to their representative sources, and (2) to transmit these impressions or representations to the sensory receptors within the bio-mind. It's possible that there exist multitudes of such receptors and channels—from cellular levels all the way up to the cognitive functions of the discerning or misjudging intellect.

And so, if the sensorial exists, we might safely assume that it exists in everyone, that everyone has a sensorial—and that everyone's sensorial is connected to their motorium, their bio-mind sensorial-motorium. We can also expect that the sensorial conveys various kinds of information to the cognitive consciousness in the form of sensations, feelings, impulses, and signals—which may or may not produce mental image pictures.

And as I have occasionally pointed out, in the end it does not matter which senses we have, or where they are located within the bio-mind framework. The only thing that matters is whether they are active or inactive—and correctly so.

But incorrect concepts held within the bio-mind intellect seem to have a great deal to do with how what functions, and why and when and IF one is aware of "representations" of everything.

Just as one cannot simply look at a bridge and expect to build one, one cannot look at the results of superpowers in others and hope to attain them without first understanding the processes and structures that go into their creation. The majestic bridges we see are the tangible outcomes of meticulous planning and arduous labor. Similarly, the extraordinary faculties displayed by some are the visible effects of underlying processes, ones which must be comprehended before attempting to harness such powers for oneself.

AS HUMAN BEINGS, WE ARE GUIDED BY A COMPLEX NETWORK OF SENSORY INPUTS THAT EXTEND BEYOND THE FIVE SENSES WE ARE TAUGHT EXIST. THESE INTRICATE MECHANISMS WORK TOGETHER TO SHAPE OUR PERCEPTION OF THE WORLD AROUND US, INFLUENCING HOW WE INTERPRET AND UNDERSTAND OUR EXPERIENCES. WHETHER ONE TYPE OF INPUT DOMINATES OVER THE OTHERS IS INCONSEQUENTIAL; WHAT TRULY MATTERS IS HOW THESE PROCESSES SHAPE OUR PERCEPTIONS AND THUS OUR INDIVIDUAL REALITIES.

WITHOUT A DEEP UNDERSTANDING OF THESE PROCESSES AND HOW THEY UNLOCK THE POTENTIAL OF OUR BIO-MIND, ANY ATTEMPTS TO UTILIZE THESE INNATE ABILITIES WILL LIKELY BE INCONSISTENT AND UNPREDICTABLE. IT IS ONLY THROUGH THIS DEEP UNDERSTANDING, GAINED THROUGH DEDICATED EFFORT AND CONSCIOUS PRACTICE, THAT WE CAN TRULY TAP INTO AND UTILIZE THE INNATE SUPERPOWERS WITHIN US.

A BioMind Superpowers Book from
Swann-Ryder Productions, LLC

www.ingoswann.com

OTHER BOOKS BY INGO SWANN

Everybody's Guide to Natural ESP
Master of Harmlessness
Penetration
Penetration: Special Edition Updated
Preserving the Psychic Child
Psychic Literacy
Psychic Sexuality
Purple Fables
Reality Boxes
Resurrecting the Mysterious
Secrets of Power, Volume 1
Secrets of Power, Volume 2
Star Fire
The Great Apparitions of Mary
The Windy Song
The Wisdom Category
Your Nostradamus Factor

www.ingramcontent.com/pod-product-compliance
Lightning Source LLC
Chambersburg PA
CBHW070108080526
44586CB00013B/1226